CULTURE OF LIES

EXPOSING COVERT STRONGHOLDS

C.L. SUTHERIN

Trilogy Christian Publishers
A Wholly Owned Subsidiary of Trinity Broadcasting Network
2442 Michelle Drive
Tustin, CA 92780

Copyright © 2024 by C.L. Sutherin

All Scripture quotations, unless otherwise noted, are taken from the Amplified® Bible (AMP), Copyright © 2015 by The Lockman Foundation. Used by permission. www.Lockman.org. Scripture quotations marked ABPE are taken from Aramaic Bible in Plain English, 2010 Copyright©, Rev. David Bauscher, Lulu Enterprises Incorporated, 2010. Scripture quotations marked "BLB" are taken from The Holy Bible, Berean Literal Bible, BLB. Copyright ©2016, 2018 by Bible Hub. Used by Permission. All Rights Reserved Worldwide. www.berean.bible Scripture quotations marked "BSB" are taken from The Holy Bible, Berean Study Bible, BSB. Copyright ©2016, 2018 by Bible Hub. Used by Permission. All Rights Reserved Worldwide. www.berean.bible Scripture quotations marked HCSB are taken from the Holman Christian Standard Bible®, Copyright © 1999, 2000, 2002, 2003 by Holman Bible Publishers. Used by permission. Scripture texts marked NAB in this work are taken from the New American Bible, revised edition © 2010, 1991, 1986, 1970 Confraternity of Christian Doctrine, Washington, D.C. and are used by permission of the copyright owner. All Rights Reserved. No part of the New American Bible may be reproduced in any form without permission in writing from the copyright owner. Scripture quotations marked NASB are taken from the New American Standard Bible® (NASB), Copyright © 1960, 1962, 1963, 1968, 1971, 1972, 1973, 1975, 1977, 1995 by The Lockman Foundation. Used by permission. www.Lockman.org. Scripture quotations marked NIV are taken from the Holy Bible, New International Version®, NIV®. Copyright © 1973, 1978, 1984, 2011 by Biblica, Inc.TM Used by permission of Zondervan. All rights reserved worldwide. www.zondervan.com. The "NIV" and "New International Version" are trademarks registered in the United States Patent and Trademark Office by Biblica, Inc.TM Scripture quotations marked NKJV are taken from the New King James Version®. Copyright © 1982 by Thomas Nelson. Used by permission. All rights reserved. Scripture quotations marked KJV are taken from the King James Version of the Bible. Public domain.

All rights reserved, including the right to reproduce this book or portions thereof in any form whatsoever.

For information, address Trilogy Christian Publishing
Rights Department, 2442 Michelle Drive, Tustin, Ca 92780.

Trilogy Christian Publishing/ TBN and colophon are trademarks of Trinity Broadcasting Network.

For information about special discounts for bulk purchases, please contact Trilogy Christian Publishing.

Trilogy Disclaimer: The views and content expressed in this book are those of the author and may not necessarily reflect the views and doctrine of Trilogy Christian Publishing or the Trinity Broadcasting Network.

10 9 8 7 6 5 4 3 2 1

Library of Congress Cataloging-in-Publication Data is available.

ISBN 979-8-89333-353-4

ISBN 979-8-89333-354-1 (ebook)

ACKNOWLEDGMENTS

Above all, I want to thank my Lord and Savior, Jesus Christ. Without Him, I probably wouldn't be around to write this book. It is through His love for me that I have put off the old me and been filled with His constant presence and power to accomplish all that He sets before me. I am forever grateful for the amazing love of God!

Secondly, I owe a big thank you to my husband, Barry, who tirelessly supports me in all of my endeavors. He never complained about the abundance of time that was needed to be alone with my Lord, seeking His guidance, and to concentrate on completing this book.

I'm also grateful to my friend Maritza, who supported this project in prayer and technical assistance, as well as my friend Roxanne, whose prayer and counsel encouraged me along to completion.

TABLE OF CONTENTS

Acknowledgments 3
Foreword.. 7
Chapter 1 - The Wandering................................... 11
Chapter 2 - The Long Road Home........................ 17
Chapter 3 - Isn't the Bible Just Another Religious Book? 43
Chapter 4 - Is Truth Relative?............................... 49
Chapter 5 - Let's Take a Look at the Occult.......... 55
Chapter 6 - The Kingdom of Satan 57
Chapter 7 - A Brief Overview of the Occult in the Bible 61
Chapter 8 - God's Miraculous Power Living Inside of You... 79
Chapter 9 - Confident Access to God's
Presence and Provision 85
Chapter 10 - Equipped for Spiritual Warfare........ 87
Chapter 11 - The Practice of Prayer and Fasting 105
Chapter 12 - The Practice of Thanksgiving,
Praise, and Worship.. 109
Chapter 13 - My Testimony 115
Chapter 14 - Finding the Common Thread........ 121

FOREWORD

As the lead pastor of LifePoint Community Church, I see the effects that dabbling in the occult can have on individual lives. In her book *Culture of Lies*, Connie Sutherin pieces together her personal life story with clear and precise facts of the dangers of the occult and how a relationship with Jesus Christ gives the Christian the power to overcome the evil that is set out to destroy our lives. Connie lays out in plain terms the way to this freedom and uses scriptures from the Bible to pave the road to victory! If you are seeking freedom in your life or are praying for a loved one to come to know Jesus personally, this book will give you the tools and encouragement you need to develop a relationship with the freedom giver, Jesus!

—Pastor Don Jagers
Lead pastor of LifePoint Community Church,
DeLand, Florida

My people are destroyed for lack of knowledge.

Hosea 4:6a (KJV)

And this I pray, that your love may overflow still more and more in real knowledge and all discernment, so that you may… be sincere and blameless for the day of Christ

Philippians 1:9–10 (NASB; emphasis added)

CHAPTER 1

The Wandering

(Uncovered)

I'm chasing the setting sun dissolving into distant canyons, washing them in shimmering hues. Struggling up onto the highest outcrop, I'm caught off guard by a blast of desert wind. It slaps my braid across my face like a whip, nearly toppling me. I scramble to secure my footing; small stones slide out from underfoot, careening to the canyon below. My heart is pounding, and I catch my breath, sucking in pungent sage and pine. My senses sent spinning like a child's kaleidoscope. I'm nearly overwhelmed with awe at the exquisiteness. My senses are awash in amazement, and it calms my pounding heart.

Scanning the adjacent cliffs to see who else has risked a climb this high, I see that no one is in sight. Just then, a resounding male voice calls out my name from somewhere below. The deep voice carries a tone of distinct earnestness, like that of someone urgently looking for me.

"Connie!"

But I can't spot anyone...

Carefully picking my way back down I realize that whoever called me had used my *given* name, Connie. This stopped me in my tracks.

I was only known to these people by my hippie name, "Sunshine."

Wow, I think to myself. *Something weird is happening here.*

Several of my hiking companions are relaxing at the picnic area below. I yell to them, "Did one of you call for me?"

"No, maybe it was George or Tera. They are still up on the lower ridge."

Reaching the picnic area, I found that no one in our group had heard what I heard.

Baffled, I can't help but ponder whose voice it was and how He knew my name as Connie. This bizarre experience somewhat freaked me out, but I soon put it to the back of my mind.

It would take a while before I was able to discover Who it actually was that had called out to me on that beautiful Spring evening.

Prayers of Believing Parents

"The earnest (heartfelt, continued) prayer of a righteous man [or woman] makes tremendous power available [dynamic in its working]" (James 5:16b; "or woman" added).

I am very blessed!

What words are sufficient to thank parents who raised you in a godly home, wrestling in prayer for you every single day?

My parents each gave their lives to Jesus Christ while attending a Billy Graham rally in the sweaty summer of 1953. At the time, my mom was three months pregnant with me. Their decision to follow Christ changed the trajectory of our family's lifestyle and destiny. Our life revolved around church, family, and service work for organizations such as the local Rescue Mission and Child Evangelism Fellowship.

During Sunday School, at the tender age of five, I took Jesus "under my shirt." Following this, I distinctly remember being baptized by immersion. Oh, how my emotions were thrilled by that lofty occasion! Although I was quite young, these experiences shined like a treasure in my heart. I remember carrying a deep sense of devotion to the One to Whom I had pledged my life. As a young child, nearly all of my life was ideal. But at the tender age of eight, everything changed.

Uncovered

What does "uncover" mean here?

Most dictionaries define a cover as something used to protect and conceal.

When danger erupts, someone might shout, "Take cover!" We cover our nakedness with clothing. Very young children are covered by their innocence and by their parents' watchfulness. So, for the sake of this particular discussion, let's say to uncover is to *expose and remove from being protected.*

Any child who has been sexually abused has experienced the uncovering of their innocence through the uncovering of their private areas (genitals), as well as a real or perceived loss of the protective covering by one's parents. Now, instead of being covered in innocence and protection, the little one is clothed in shame. This produces feelings of being exposed, betrayed, unprotected, and unloved. Fear is not far behind.

This is what it means for a child to be uncovered, and this is tragic!

At the impressionable age of eight, a thorny seed of grief and rage took root in the soil of my heart. This dreadful root was festering in my vulnerable soul following a series of sexual assaults by a neighbor. He was a man whom my parents knew and trusted.

This horrible man threatened violence against my mom if I told anyone of his abuse, and because he shamed me (telling me I was responsible), I never disclosed the assaults to anyone. I buried it in a forgotten closet of my memory. However, these malignant attacks seared themselves deep into my psyche, thrusting my life on a trajectory of self-destruction and rebellion, driven by rage and shame. Every important decision I made was distorted by my damaged view of the world and myself.

This is what happens to many children who have been sexually exploited.

I developed a firmly rooted belief that my value hinged *only* upon my ability to "perform for," please, or impress others. I recognized no other value in myself. This belief mushroomed as I grew into adulthood. I was seldom able to be genuine with anyone in my intimate relationships. This ultimately destroyed or seriously wounded all of them. Furthermore, the damage to my personality produced in me a feeling of worthlessness. This affected how I carried myself, and I was easily spotted by those who were always searching for their next victim. Adding to those risks, as I matured, my romantic desires were always toward men who carried that "bad boy" persona. The outcome of this distorted life-view, the buried rage and grief eventually manifested into dangerous territory. Without even recognizing what was taking place, I became subconsciously bent on self-destruction.

My high school years were marked by the Vietnam War and the explosion of a social upheaval known as the New Age movement, as well as the sexual revolution. So many were in rebellion against so many ideologies and traditions! The defiant nature of this era drew me into its vortex like a fallen leaf in a whirlpool! The rebel in me was captivated by the revolutionary nature of that period. I was enamored with the Age of Aquarius. Even though the current events of my high school years fascinated me, I held to most of my Judeo-Christian beliefs and standards.

Despite this, I felt helpless to resist the magnetic lure of sexual experimentation with my high school sweetheart. His attention and affection were an irresistible draw to my confused heart. I savored his interest and affection, so I allowed his sexual advances in hopes that I pleased him, ensuring that he would not discard me. I became pregnant and was married just before graduating high school. Before two years were out, I was pregnant again with our second son.

The birthing process was difficult for our first child, so I decided to try the Lamaze natural childbirth method, which is a form of focused breathing and focused meditation to overcome the challenge and pain of childbirth. I was clueless that I was practicing a form of *Eastern mysticism*. This ritual would lead me deeper into occult activity.

It's no surprise that I soon also took up yoga at the YMCA and practiced it daily. Had I known what paths this practice would lead me to, I would like to think that I wouldn't have chosen to explore them, but I was young, rebellious, and oh, so naive! I had no understanding of the deeper, dark spiritual connection that was attached to what I was chasing or the power over my thinking that was taking place. This path of life was not leading to spiritual enlightenment, but to a dark and dangerous highway. My life spiraled downward. I started feeling incapable of safely parenting my two sons while simultaneously feeling powerless to change.

By this time, my sons were two and four years old. I had moved us two thousand miles west, and we were living in a hippie commune-type neighborhood in the mountains of Arizona. My heart was torn because I knew my lifestyle was neither safe nor beneficial for my boys, yet I felt completely powerless to change what I was doing. This contradiction between my behavior and my intentions brought me to the decision to take my children back to their father (who wanted custody all along due to my life choices). The boys and I returned to Florida, where they would live with their father and stepmother and only a few miles from other extended family. I told myself that they were safe and in good hands. I didn't want to think about how broken my heart was. I pushed the pain down and down.

I returned to Arizona by myself... all alone (or so I thought).

Once I was back in Arizona, I plummeted even deeper into the New Age movement, experimenting with mysticism, telekinesis, Native American animism, mind-altering drugs, and other dark experiences. For over two years, I even hitchhiked all around the continental United States. I nearly always traveled with my dog or a companion, but neither could protect me. There's absolutely no doubt in my mind that it was God's sovereign hand of protection keeping me, or I would be dead... (More on this later.)

During this time, cell phones were unheard of (except for those depicted in shows about outer space). The only communication with my parents was through letters and occasional calls from pay phones. I was rarely able to speak with my sons. Their father and his wife refused my calls. This was a source of mental anguish washing over me like a raging sea, driving me down and down! Missing my sons and the guilt of leaving them so far away jettisoned me deeper into a chaotic lifestyle. I started drinking heavily to dull the internal turmoil. Even that didn't work. *I was running away from everything, including myself!*

My parents were extremely concerned for my physical and spiritual well-being, but they prayed for me daily. *I later found out that my dear mom had even made a specific request to the Lord… to go to me and call me out* by my name! Whose was the voice that I heard calling out to me from the precipice of those cliffs? It was the very first and only time that I have experienced the immense privilege of audibly hearing from the Lord. Though after surrendering myself fully to God, He often has spoken to me through Scripture and in a still, small voice deep in my heart. The experience on the cliff was unique in that it was a voice coming through my ear.

Whether it was Jesus Himself or one of His angelic messengers sent to rouse my wandering soul back home, I can't say for sure. But I know that I heard a loud, clear male voice calling me by a name that no others (who were currently in my life) ever knew. *It was only a year or so later that I realized that God's voice and my longing heart were drawing this prodigal home into the arms of Jesus!*

CHAPTER 2
The Long Road Home

Vicki, McBarker, and I hitchhiked to Yakima, Washington, where we met up with Mary. We easily found the promise of work from the same orchard owner I had picked for the previous year. We set ourselves up in a migrant shack near the Naches River. This was my second season of migrant work in Washington. Working in the fresh air and sunshine, we spent our days climbing and sweating and our evenings drinking beer in a little tavern on the river.

Several weeks before the end of apple season, I received a Bible in the mail. I hadn't asked for it, but my mom and dad shipped it to me. Well aware they hoped that I would read it, I stared intently at the Bible in my hands for a few minutes. Feeling compelled to open its pages. I randomly opened the book of Psalms. As I thumbed through it, several familiar passages jumped out at me, causing my heart to soar and tears to well up. Then I found verses in the New Testament I'd never noticed before about Jesus having authority over demons that were tormenting people, driving the demons out. To my amazement, I even discovered in Luke 10 that Jesus sent seventy-two disciples ahead of Him. Using His Name, and *by the authority of His Name,* even His disciples were casting demons out! In all my childhood church attendance, I had never heard such things. This all amazed and excited me. Something happened to me right then and there.

After that day, I found myself eager for the next opportunity to read the Bible and refamiliarize myself with the Lord from Whom I had wandered. Almost suddenly, I no longer felt so distant. Going to the tavern in the evenings lost its appeal. Instead, I found myself combing the pages of the Bible, discovering fresh meaning and revelation in passages that I had previously never known! I knew God was doing a work in my heart because I started praying and asked God for His forgiveness. For the first time in a long while, I yearned to return to Florida near my family and children. I didn't feel estranged anymore, and I wanted to be with the people who love me!

Soon after receiving the Bible, I headed to the pay phone outside the bar and called home. It was early morning in Yakima (three hours later In Florida). I figured my mother would answer. I was surprised to hear my younger brother's voice on the other end.

"Hello?"

"Dave. It's Connie."

"Conn, it's you!" came his reply. Just then, the phone clatters as the receiver crashes to the kitchen counter, and I hear my brother hollering down the hallway, "Mom, Mom, Connie's on the phone."

Mom picked up in her bedroom. "Connie, you never call before work. Is everything all right?"

"Mom, I'm not going to pick apples today because I'm heading home to see you and be near my boys. Is it all right if I stay with you and Dad until I get a job and place of my own?"

There was total silence on the other end for a moment.

"Mom, are you still there?" Then came her beautiful reply, the sound of my mother softly weeping.

"Mom, are you okay?"

"I'm just crying because I'm happy and relieved. But what made you decide to come home?"

The answer was easy for me to see.

"I've been reading the Bible you and Dad sent me, and it made me realize that I need to come home and keep getting closer to God." Now, my mom was full-on crying and thanking

God between joyful cries. Of course, her joyful tears brought me to the same delight!

It was a sacred moment. Mommy and I wept together, a moment of healing and reconciliation that felt all-encompassing and sweet as the summer rain! Once we calmed down a little, Mom offered to check with Dad and see if they could afford a ticket to fly home.

"No, Mom, that's too much. I'll just—"

Mom cut me off mid-sentence. "Well, at least a bus ticket. I know we can swing that."

"No, thank you; I'm not about to leave my friend, McBarker, behind. After all, that dog has been my traveling buddy for nearly two years. Just pray me home."

Pray is what they did, and thank God! I had a three-thousand-mile voyage to Florida and another immeasurable quest to the center of God's will for my life. Both journeys were messy and dangerous, but God does not leave us defenseless. Hallelujah!

"Behold, I am with you and will keep [careful watch over you and guard] you wherever you may go, and I will bring you back to this [promised] land; for I will not leave you until I have done what I have promised you" (Genesis 28:15).

With the backpack secured, McBarker and I headed out the following morning, hitchhiking to Union Gap, where we picked up I-82 East, toward Stanfield, and then onward, via I-84 East, to Twin Falls, Idaho, where we pitched our tent in the dusk of evening. We were in a state park just a few miles off the interstate. A whip-poor-will claimed his perch with a lovely night song, blending beautifully with the rhythm of the crickets. Like a gentle lullaby, we drifted to sleep, McBarker gently snoring. The next morning, we were on the road by daybreak. The rest of our trip was uneventful until we hit South Carolina. That's where I encountered proof positive that demons are real, but the power in the *Name of Jesus* is also very real and the *most powerful of all!*

Satan Unobserved

I saw him look over at me when his car whizzed by, sending a cloud of gravel flying as he pulled over, skidding to a stop (his car was about two hundred feet from me). I flung my backpack over one shoulder. McBarker got up and followed at a trot.

"Hey, thanks for stopping."

"Where are you headed?" he asked as he looked at McBarker.

"Florida, Daytona Beach." I bent over and looked him in the eyes. He seemed harmless enough, and McBarker's hackles weren't up so I thought I might take a chance on riding with him.

"Your whole back seat is covered in tools; can you make room for my dog? Where are you going?" I asked.

"Sure, hang on," he answered as he climbed out of the car. "I can take you as far as Greenville." He moved most of his equipment to the trunk, and I tossed my backpack into the back seat with McBarker, got in the passenger seat, and off we went.

"My name's Larry."

"I'm Sunshine, and this here is McBarker." McBarker barked when I said his name. Larry almost jumped through the roof.

"He doesn't bite, does he?"

"Not unless you tried to hurt me or something."

"Well, I guess it'll be all right then; tell him to lay down, though, so he's not breathing in my ear."

"Lay down, boy." Larry pulled away as McBarker sniffed his ear. Then, McBarker settled down for a nap. We were about six hours from Greenville, so I figured I'd strike up a conversation to pass the time.

"Do you work in construction?" (The tools he had moved gave the clue.)

"Yeah, I'm on the last couple of weeks of a project in Greensville, and then I'm going down to Jacksonville for another job that just started up. I have a buddy leaving for Florida tonight. I'll give him a call later and see if you can ride with him."

"Wow, that would be great," I answered, thinking that this was turning out to be one of the easiest hitchhiking trips I had experienced.

"What's in Daytona Beach?" Larry inquired.

"Oh, my parents live there. I've been up in Washington picking apples, so now I'm heading to my folks to stay with them for a while."

"Picking apples; why are you picking apples?"

"Because you can make around two hundred dollars a day."

"Dang! That's not bad money."

"Yeah, the orchard owner I worked for even lets you stay in a small house on his property for free. I was up there with a couple of friends, making some pretty good money. The season's over now, though."

Our small talk continued between stretches of silence until we reached the outskirts of Greenville, where he pulled into a small market's parking lot next to a pay phone.

Shutting the engine down, Larry explained, "I'm calling my guy who's leaving for Florida tonight to see if he'll let you ride along. There's a clean bathroom inside this place if you need it."

Larry was still on the phone when I came out. McBarker sniffed around and relieved himself. I noticed Larry hung up, climbing back into his car, so I hurried back, whistling for McBarker to come.

"So, good news; Rick said you're welcome to ride along to Jacksonville later tonight, but he's not leaving till nine o'clock, so we have some time to kill. You wanna get something to eat?"

"Sure, but I need to let my dog eat first. I carry his food and bowl, but he won't eat in the car."

Larry drove us to the room he was renting, where we left McBarker. He must have needed a break from traveling, making himself at home; he hopped onto one of the twin beds. I put food and water out for him, and we left to find something for our rumbly bellies.

"What are you hungry for?" Larry asked as we pulled out of the motel parking lot.

"I don't care, as long as it's cheap. I sent most of my money home to my folks."

We swung into the drive-through of a local hamburger dive, loading up on burgers, fries, a chocolate shake, and soda for Larry. I pulled out some cash to give him, but he waved me off.

"Thanks, man. I wasn't expecting that."

Larry just nodded. "I need to run by this guy's house to see if he has any reefer. Do you need any?"

"Nope, I'm good, thank you."

We drove across town, listening to the news on some radio station. I was surprised and a little worried to hear the weather report about Hurricane David making landfall this very day in Florida. I wondered if the hurricane would throw a wrench on my ride to Florida that night and was a little worried about my folks. But my dad knew how to prepare for hurricanes. It was nothing new to him.

Taking Highway 29 North, through some rural backwoods, and crossing over Brushy Creek, we turned down into a driveway leading to a run-down mobile home. Larry banged on the screen door, which was answered by a woman still in her bathrobe. The two exchanged conversation on the porch, and then Larry came back to the car.

"Well, Charlie just went to pick up some more pot, so we'll come back in an hour. Let's head back to that creek we just crossed; I wanna show you something."

"What?"

"Bow fishing."

"You mean fishing with a bow and arrow?"

"Yup, I'm pretty good at it too."

"Okay, show me," I answered, since I had never even heard of bow fishing, but only hunting game with a bow and arrow.

We drove back to the bridge, parked on the embankment, and made our way to the water's edge. Larry tossed some rolled-up balls of bread into a calm part of the creek and stood poised with his bow and arrow, but no fish were going for it. One by one, the balls of bread just sank. He threw out a few more pieces, and the same thing happened. Larry set his bow down and headed for his car.

"Hey, where are you going?" I hollered after him.

"I just remembered some meat scraps I have in a jar from the other day when I was fishing," he yelled back.

I watched as he reached into the floorboard of his back seat to retrieve something that I assumed was a container of meat scraps and then headed back down the hill to where he left his bow. After flinging the little chunks of meat into the water, Larry came and stood right next to me, I mean right in my personal space, putting his arm around my shoulder.

"Hey, it's pretty private out here," he crooned. "What do you say we have a little fun and fool around? I've got a sleeping bag we can stretch out on the grass."

Instant fear and trepidation erupted in my chest, but I told myself not to show it. Gently pulling my shoulder out from under his hand, I looked him straight in the eye, stating with a very firm tone, "Larry, I'm not the kind of girl to go sleeping around with someone I just met, so if that's what you're looking for, let's head back to town so that I can get my dog and backpack. Then you can just go to the bar or something. Maybe you'll get lucky there, but not with me! Besides, I *really* want to find out more about Hurricane David and call my parents to check on them, so let's just go."

With that, I turned and headed back toward the car. I could hear Larry coming behind me, catching up with me just as I turned to climb the embankment. At just that moment, I felt a thud, with a huge explosion of pain at the top of my head, seeing stars. The next thing I knew, I was flat on my back, looking up at Larry, who was straddling me, sitting on my chest.

"Now you will," he demanded.

"No, I won't!" I shouted back at him.

He slapped me hard, knocking my glasses into the bushes. Next, he held a knife up over my face, with his arm raised for a strike.

"I rebuke the devil in you, in the *Name of Jesus*," I commanded, staring right into the face of *not* Larry but some horrible, demonic image superimposed over his features.

He instantly lowered the knife, putting his *finger* over my lips as if to hush me.

"Don't say that," he begged me in a high, shrill whisper that sounded less than human.

I moved his finger. "I rebuke the devil in you, in the Name of Jesus!" I shouted back at him.

He sat up with a jerk, and instantly, his normal features returned to his face.

"Oh no," he cried. "Look what I've done; you're bleeding. What can I do?"

"Give me the knife," I told him firmly. He complied. "Now, please find my glasses in the bushes."

While he searched, I spotted a hammer with my blood on it. I grabbed that and got up from the ground.

"Found them, but they're bent; I'm so sorry, so sorry!"

"Larry, you need to take me back to town."

"Yeah, okay, I'll take you back."

We got back into his car and pulled onto the highway, headed back to town. It was about a twenty-minute drive. Not once did Larry ask me not to tell anyone what he did. Instead, the whole way back, he asked me questions, one after the other, about the Bible and what happened when I rebuked the devil in him. All he kept saying was that he had injured his head not long ago in a serious car wreck, and he'd never been the same since. That "something" would suddenly come over him. Then he would apologize again, so I told him I forgave him. We were nearly back to his hotel.

"Will you hang out and tell me some more about God and Jesus? I won't hurt you again, I promise."

"If you sincerely want to learn more about Jesus, you need to find a church, like a Baptist church, and go there. I'm going to head on down the road and find a place to get cleaned up. I'm sure you understand."

"Yeah, I do. I didn't mean to scare you off. I'm sorry."

I retrieved a clean bandana and wrapped it around my bleeding skull, gathered up my dog and belongings, and left with barely a goodbye.

I didn't know where I was heading, so I wandered down the avenue looking for a pay phone to call someone for help. There's a hotel ahead with a pay phone in the entryway, so I tied McBarker to the light pole, went in, and opened the phone directory, hanging there. I first tried the rectory of a local church, but after hearing my story, whoever was on the other end said, "Sorry, we can't help you," and hung up.

Astonished that I couldn't find help from a church and not knowing what else to do, I called my mom, hating that she would have to find out about this harrowing experience over the phone. It sorrowed me to upset my parents with this news, but my mom was a rock. She rallied, assuring me that everything was going to be okay, asking how badly I was injured. I told her that I didn't know because, at that moment, I didn't know that I would later require twelve stitches in my scalp and also underneath my scalp. Mom advised me to call the police, so I did.

Police report filed, I was dropped off at The Salvation Army, where the director and his wife took me to the hospital, then back to the center to rest, as per doctor's orders, for three days. These wonderful people even cared for McBarker in their home while I recuperated.

My parents again offered me a bus ticket, but as before, I refused to leave McBarker behind.

"Well, we will just pray you and McBarker home," was Mom's reply, and this time, I had absolute faith that I would make it home just fine.

The next morning, the director's wife dropped me and McBarker near the I-95 South ramp. There was a coffee shop there, so I secured McBarker to a bench outside the entry and went in for a cup. Just as I was served, a guy in a suit walked past me with an armload of cardboard, settling into a booth near the restrooms. Now, if you've never hitchhiked, you might not understand the value of a nice cardboard placard decorated with the name of your destination in big, bold letters. It can be your ticket to the longest ride heading toward your destination. I finished my coffee and headed toward the restroom.

Stopping at his booth, I asked, "Can you spare one of those pieces of cardboard, Mister?"

The guy looked up from his notebook and just stared at me, mouth agape. I giggled at how silly he looked, and he blushed.

"Huh? Why do you want a piece of cardboard?"

"No, me first. Why are you carrying around cardboard?"

"I sell cardboard. Now you."

"Okay, I need it to make a sign showing my destination."

"Your destination?"

"Yes, I'm hitchhiking to Florida, my dog and me."

"Your dog, tied up outside?"

"Yes"

"Hmm, if your dog is friendly, you're in luck."

"Why?" I said, leaning a little closer.

"Because when I leave here, I'm heading for Ormond Beach, Florida, and you are welcome to ride along, as well as your pooch."

I thought I was going to kiss this guy, but all I did was laugh out loud with joy.

"I'm headed to my parent's home, just south of Daytona Beach."

"Better yet, I'll just take you to their front door; how's that?"

I looked upward and said, "Thank You, Lord!"

My journey to the heart of God's will for me was fraught with pitfalls and distractions sent by Satan and roused by my own flesh and stubborn independence. The previous occult activity was not something from which I was immediately extracted. Because as a young child, I put my faith in Jesus, I was not *possessed* by demons. Possession speaks of ownership, and *I belong to Christ*, but I certainly was oppressed and heavily under the influence of demonic powers. After all, I had opened the door of my life and mind through participation in occult activity. It was an intense uphill fight against the enemy of my soul.

Tragically, Satan had blinded my spiritual eyes and erected destructive strongholds in my life.

Yes, Jesus was right there inside of me, and His love was abundant, but my rebellion had broken our fellowship, and I lacked the insight to know how to recognize or receive from Him. My self-loathing blinded me to His love and grace. I felt cut off! The *consequences* of involvement with the occult are not something easily shaken. Demons that are associated with every occultic activity (no matter how innocent it seems) will wrap ugly talons around your mind, battling to hang on. Perhaps prayers of spiritual deliverance would have brought me more immediate relief, but that is not how rescue happened to me. Instead, it was long, staggering progress. Pressing into Jesus, longing for more, stumbling, getting up again, and drawing nearer to Jesus. All the while, knowing something was missing, but later realizing that it was this: I couldn't apprehend the immensity of God's love for me in such a way as to receive it. It was currently a seed, waiting in parched ground.

Here's the truth: It *is the power of God's love that strengthens us against temptation, and refines us throughout our journey with God.*

Here's the good news: once my heart was softened, I *did taste and experience the great love of Jesus.* I was able to let Him heal and renew my battered soul. I came to realize that I had, up until then, no idea what love was really about. When the healing of my heart began, I finally grasped and relished the genuine, unconditional, and healing love that Jesus pours out on everyone who comes to Him. I'm sorry to say that it took years for me to finally allow Jesus to break off all of the chains that bound me. I tried to shake them off myself. No human can win against Satan in their limited human power. Trying to "get it right" is exactly why it took me so long to find peace and rest in God. I just couldn't maintain any consistency when trying through my limited efforts. It's the power of God's love that renews my life, softening out all the rough edges and finally bringing sweet liberty from the chains of Satan's lies.

Listen to what the Bible says about fighting the enemy, Satan, and his demonic hosts.

> For our struggle is not against flesh and blood [contending only with physical opponents], but against the rulers, against the powers, against the world forces of this [present] darkness, against the spiritual *forces* of wickedness in the heavenly (supernatural) *places*.
>
> Ephesians 6:12

Did the levity of the verse above open the eyes of your heart to the futility of fighting Satan's kingdom by the strength of your unregenerated flesh? *Impossible on your own!* Here is what God is looking for and exactly what will bring you to victory against the gates of Hell. God will work this in you if you set your heart on a hot pursuit after His will and way (making your relationship with Him the number one priority in your life).

- First and foremost, you must be *born again* from on high.
- "Jesus answered him, 'I assure you *and* most solemnly say to you, unless a person is born again [reborn from above—spiritually transformed, renewed, sanctified],

he cannot [ever] see *and* experience the kingdom of God'" (John 3:3).
- Next, *finally* yielding your rebellious heart *fully* to Father God, holding Him in awe and reverential fear.
- Genuine repentance for past decisions and actions taken without first seeking God's will *and* waiting for His answer.
- Ask for and receive the infilling of Holy Spirit, Who is the perfect teacher of God's will and way. Holy Spirit will bring you into all truth, showing you how to recognize the enemy (see the first three chapters of the book of Acts for further explanation of the infilling of Holy Spirit).
- Daily study of the Bible and memorization of various key passages, asking Holy Spirit to teach you when you are studying the Bible.

But the Helper (Comforter, Advocate, Intercessor—Counselor, Strengthener, Standby), the Holy Spirit, whom the Father will send in My name [in My place, to represent Me and act on My behalf], He will teach you all things. And He will help you remember everything that I have told you.

John 14:26

Holy Spirit will bring necessary verses to your mind just when you need them as weapons against the attacks of the enemy (but you must first hide them in your heart before these scriptures can be retrieved by Holy Spirit).
- Developing a prayer life, which includes thanksgiving, praise, and worship, as well as asking for and receiving the guidance of Holy Spirit (more on this in pages to come).
- Learn about and participate in a fast unto God (more on this in chapters to follow).

I'm amazed at how long I remained in the shadows of misunderstanding God's awesome power and great love for me! I had no idea *and certainly* was ignorant of how to personally experience that love and power in my life! Throughout this metamorphosis, I stumbled hard…repeatedly! I was a mess before I surrendered fully. My *self-will run riot* made the journey of achieving liberty and *rest with God* longer and far more difficult than was necessary. But throughout the entire crossing, Jesus was always right there, whether I knew it or not, meeting me at every twist and turn, certainly saving my life more times than I care to ponder. His compassionate grace and love empowered me to continue pressing in, with Holy Spirit patiently pointing the way.

In all my seeking and all my yearning, all my stumbling and rising, there was Jesus, just waiting for me to turn around!

The pain and struggle of getting free is what motivates me to write this book for you. I pray that you'll keep turning the pages, perhaps saving yourself from a similarly long and painful journey. Fellow believers: Brothers and Sisters, I pray that the information and warnings of this book come through loud enough. Will you heed the call of Holy Spirit shouting, "Wake up, the bridegroom is at the gate!"

> For if we believe that Jesus died and rose again [as in fact He did], even so God [in this same way—by raising them from the dead] will bring with Him those [believers] who have fallen asleep in Jesus. For we say this to you by the Lord's [own] word, that we who are still alive and remain until the coming of the Lord, will in no way precede [into His presence] those [believers] who have fallen asleep [in death]. For the Lord Himself will come down from heaven with a shout of command, with the voice of the archangel and with the [blast of the] trumpet of God, and the dead in Christ will rise first. Then we who are alive and remain [on the earth] will simultaneously be caught up (raptured) together with

them [the resurrected ones] in the clouds to meet the Lord in the air, and so we will always be with the Lord!

1 Thessalonians 4:14–17

Beloved, are you one who unknowingly (or even willfully) dabbles in or fully participates in occult activities, such as astrology (reading your horoscope), tarot cards, consulting psychics, streaming videos or shows about witchcraft, demonic and worldly ideas or activities? Do you tell yourself it's just for fun and entertainment? *My heart's cry for you is that you will prayerfully consider all that is laid out in the pages to follow.*

Scripture clearly warns that in the last days, *many will be deceived.*

> For the time will come when people will not tolerate sound doctrine and accurate instruction [that challenges them with God's truth]; but wanting to have their ears tickled [with something pleasing], they will accumulate for themselves [many] teachers [one after another, chosen] to satisfy their own desires and to support the errors they hold, and will turn their ears away from the truth and will wander off into myths and man-made fictions [and will accept the unacceptable].
>
> 2 Timothy 4:3–4

These are Jesus' own words:

> For false Christs and false prophets will appear and they will provide great signs and wonders, so as to deceive, if possible, even the elect (God's chosen ones). Listen carefully, I have told you in advance. So if they say to you, 'Look! He is in the wilderness,' do not go out there, or, 'Look! He is in the inner rooms [of a house],' do not believe it.
>
> Matthew 24:24–26

One of Satan's most deviant methods of deception is taking what is dangerous to your soul and embellishing it *just enough* (dressing it up in something exciting or entertaining) so that you are not even *aware* of the vile flock of demons circling overhead! *Is this happening to you?*

The Bible tells us in *2 Corinthians 11:14* that *Satan disguises himself as an angel of light!* Do you think you are too clever for Satan's illusions? Have you forgotten that Satan has been around longer than we humans? Do you realize that Satan is a *supernatural creature* capable of performing supernatural feats through those who do his bidding? Here is just one example:

> Now the Lord said to Moses and Aaron, "When Pharaoh says to you, 'Work a miracle [to prove your authority],' then you say to Aaron, 'Take your staff and throw it down before Pharaoh, so that it may become a serpent.'" So Moses and Aaron came to Pharaoh, and did just as the Lord had commanded; Aaron threw down his staff before Pharaoh and his servants, and it became a serpent. Then Pharaoh called for the wise men [skilled in magic and omens] and the sorcerers [skilled in witchcraft], and they also, these magicians (soothsayer-priests) of Egypt, did the same with their secret arts and enchantments. For every man threw down his staff and they turned into serpents; but Aaron's staff swallowed up their staffs. Yet Pharaoh's heart was hardened and he would not listen to them, just as the Lord had said.
>
> Exodus 7:8–13

Satan also has thousands of years of experience observing humans, learning how to use our behavior, perception, and tendencies against us, and it's to his advantage. He is the evil master of psychology, only he aims to muddle your mind, not to heal it. His dark kingdom includes numerous demonic angels and evil spirits ready to do his bidding (Luke 11:14). Satan's realm consists of variously ranked beings who *supernaturally impact* earthly rulers, kingdoms, and territories.

Daniel, an Old Testament Prophet, was seeking God's direction. For twenty-one days, he humbled himself by fasting and praying. The answer was immediately dispatched to be delivered by an archangel of God's kingdom, but it took twenty-one days to arrive.

> On the twenty-fourth day of the first month, as I was standing on the bank of the great river, the Tigris, I lifted up my eyes, and behold, there was a certain man dressed in linen, with a belt of fine gold from Uphaz around his waist. His body was like beryl, his face like the brilliance of lightning, his eyes like flaming torches, his arms and legs like the gleam of polished bronze, and his voice like the sound of a multitude.
>
> Daniel 10:4–6 (BSB)

Daniel fell as if dead at the sight of this being but was revived to receive the sacred message.

> Suddenly, a hand touched me and set me trembling on my hands and knees. He said to me, "Daniel, you are a man who is highly precious. Consider carefully the words that I am about to say to you. Stand up, for I have now been sent to you."
>
> And when he had said this to me, I stood up trembling.
>
> "Do not be afraid, Daniel," he said, "for from the first day that you purposed to understand and to humble yourself before your God, your words were heard, and I have come in response to them. However, *the prince of the kingdom of Persia* opposed me for twenty-one days. Then Michael, one of the chief princes, came to help me, for I had been left there with the *kings of Persia*. Now I have come to explain to you what will happen to your people in the latter days, for the vision concerns those days."
>
> As he spoke with me, I was strengthened and said, "Speak, my lord, for you have strengthened me."
>
> "Do you know why I have come to you?" he said. "I must return at once to fight against the *prince of Persia*, and when I have gone forth, behold, the *prince of Greece* will come. But first I will tell you what is inscribed in the Book of Truth. Yet

no one has the courage to support me against these, except Michael your prince."

Daniel 10:10–14, 19–21 (BSB; emphasis added)

The message sent to Daniel spoke of ominous events yet to come, some of which have not yet been fulfilled. The importance of this message to the whole earth cannot be understated but must be left for another time.

The reason we are examining these scriptures in Daniel is to demonstrate the existence of Satan's evil kingdom that is highly organized and flush with supernatural influence over all of the earth.

Satan hates the Saints of God with a seething vengeance! Whether you're aware of it or not, every follower of Jesus is in an epic battle with Satan and his army of dreadful cohorts.

Ignoring this fact will never exclude you from the war!

Ephesians 6:10–13 (emphasis added) is crystal clear on this point:

> In conclusion, be strong in the Lord [draw your strength from Him and be empowered through your union with Him] and in the power of His [boundless] might. Put on the *full armor of God* [for His precepts are like the splendid armor of a heavily-armed soldier], so that you may be able to [successfully] stand up against all the schemes and the strategies and the deceits of the devil. *For our struggle* is not against flesh and blood [contending only with physical opponents], *but against the rulers, against the powers, against the world forces of this [present] darkness, against the spiritual forces of wickedness in the heavenly (supernatural) places.* Therefore, put on the complete *armor of God*, so that you will be able to [successfully] resist and stand your ground in the evil day [of danger].

Ephesians 6 also describes the devil as *a roaring lion who is seeking whom he may devour.* Far better to know your enemy and familiarize yourself with his dreadful schemes. I implore you to increase this knowledge and make use of the superior tactics and dynamic weapons of warfare provided to *His followers* by our *King Jesus, Lord God Almighty*!

God did not leave us defenseless. Hallelujah!

Romans 6:10–11 tells us that *those who put their trust in and rely completely on Jesus are indwelled by the same power that raised Him from the dead!*

Read that again!

Now, the mention of God's immense power in and through His followers brings me to my most important set of questions:

Have you put your trust in this powerful God, and do you rely on His Son, Jesus, as the Savior of your soul? Do you know that Jesus bore the entire weight of your guilt and shame on Himself when He died on the cross? Then He carried it all away! You don't have to bear that burden any longer! Are you weary from the weight of your sin? Everyone sins; you, me… *everyone. It's not important what kind of sin. Sin is part and parcel of our unregenerated human nature.*

The Bible defines sin as follows: "So any person who knows what is right to do but does not do it, to him it is sin" (James 4:17).

And there's the following: "Everyone who commits (*practices*) sin is guilty of lawlessness; for [that is what] sin is, lawlessness (the breaking, violating of God's law by transgression or neglect—being unrestrained and unregulated by His commands and His will)" (1 John 3:4; emphasis added).

God is all that is holy.

God *is* holiness! No sin can stand or enter into the presence of such divine holiness. We must find the remedy for our guilt. Therein lies the dilemma because no one can ever be good enough. We are *all* guilty of at least one sin in our lives (and, in reality, many sins). But God knew in advance that we would need someone to provide the perfect, sinless sacrifice to rescue us from ourselves and our enemy, Satan. Because of His great grace, God provided the remedy before ever creating the world.

He planned to redeem us from the curse of sin by sending His very own *sinless* Son, *Jesus*, to carry our sin and shame on Himself. *Jesus* paid the ultimate redemption price (His life), setting all who turn to Him free from the chains of sin and its ultimate consequence: physical death, eternal spiritual death, and separation from God. That eternal remedy is none other than *Jesus Christ, the Spotless Lamb of God.*

O, glory! He did not leave us as orphans but made the way through the Blood of His Son!

God doesn't desire that you pay your debt throughout eternity (steeped in misery and suffering). Jesus paid it all through His death, burial, and resurrection. He has *conquered* sin and *eternal* separation from God (eternal spiritual death). Restoration to our original intimacy with Creator God is only possible by putting your trust in what Jesus did for you through His death and resurrection. You don't have to wait any longer to be free! Just turn right now and present your life to Him. He will by no means send you away! God loves you and longs for you to be His child. He made provision for all of creation to be redeemed and has no desire to send *anyone* to Hell! Those who wind up there are going by their own decision of rejecting the gift of salvation, freely offered in love.

"The Lord does not delay [as though He were unable to act] and is not slow about His promise, as some count slowness, but is [extraordinarily] patient toward you, not wishing for any to perish but for all to come to repentance" (2 Peter 3:9).

That's why He made the way for everyone to have eternal life in His kingdom through *Jesus Christ, His Son.*

"For God so [greatly] loved and dearly prized the world, that He [even] gave His [One and] only begotten Son, so that whoever believes and trusts in Him [as Savior] shall not perish, but have eternal life" (John 3:16).

It's only those who refuse to accept His gift of salvation that are destined to an eternity separated from God and all that is good.

Imagine being in this situation, all the while knowing you would have been saved from this torment by just putting your faith in God's love for you and His plan for your good! *No one is promised tomorrow. The next breath taken could be your very last. Please! Don't wait until it's too late to turn to God and ask His forgiveness!*

You don't have to clean yourself up to turn to Jesus. He wants you just the way you are… He *prefers* you that way! But He loves you too much to leave you the same way He finds you. He will take you on a journey of changing you from the inside out. When you trust in Jesus and what He did for you through His death and resurrection, *God's Holy Spirit moves into your body.* He takes residence there and adds to your life His power and love. It's His love living and growing inside of you that brings change, not your feeble human efforts.

> Now it is God who establishes and confirms us [in joint fellowship] with you in Christ, and who has anointed us [empowering us with the gifts of the Spirit]; it is He who has also put His seal on us [that is, He has appropriated us and certified us as His] and has given us the [Holy] Spirit in our hearts as a pledge [like a security deposit to guarantee the fulfillment of His promise of eternal life].
>
> 2 Corinthians 1:21–22

You don't need anything to surrender to Jesus; just turn around. He's been waiting there all along. Just talk to Him and tell Him you want to turn away from your sin and ask His forgiveness. *He is faithful to forgive!*

No sin you have ever committed is bigger than God's grace and love for you. That's why He sent His one and only Son, *Jesus,* into our world as a human to take the punishment for your sins. And *Jesus* would have still come even if you were the only human that had ever needed saving! His love and forgiveness are very personal to your every need! But His forgiveness is not yours automatically.

You must desire and receive this gift as your *very own*.

"If we confess our sins, He is faithful and just to forgive us our sins and to cleanse us from all unrighteousness" (1 John 1:9, NKJV).

He will pick you up and set your feet on solid ground, bringing you to people and situations that transport you into new insights and amazing perspectives that have never before occurred to you. He will remove the full weight of shame off of you and carry it away. His love will cover you and restore your relationship with your *Creator, Father God*, bringing fulfillment to a yearning that you have never before been able to put your finger on. *Jesus is* the fulfillment of that yearning!

Are you aware of and *acquainted with* the power of the *Lord God, Creator* of all that is? That same power can dwell inside of you! If you give yourself to Him, that is exactly what you will discover. His unmatchable power, wisdom, and love. It is yours for the asking!

"And you will seek Me and find Me, when you search for Me with all your heart" (Jeremiah 29:13, NKJV).

Carefully consider the current state of affairs on this planet. Which of us living in today's world would refuse the gift of all the power and wisdom needed to successfully navigate life in its present condition? Everyone needs the love of Jesus (His very presence inside) to secure and encourage you on your journey. Give *God* your whole heart, and He will fill you with His *Holy Spirit*, bringing you to completion, purpose, and passion!

"The Spirit is the guarantee [the first installment, the pledge, a foretaste] of our inheritance until the redemption of God's own [purchased] possession [His believers], to the praise of His glory" (Ephesians 1:14).

Who wouldn't want the peace, power, and wisdom of *God* flowing through you like a mighty river? Don't turn away; turn *around* and start your journey to heights you've never dreamed of through peace with *Father God*. Do it today, my friend!

> Things which the eye has not seen and the ear has not heard, And which have not entered the heart of man, All that God has prepared for those who love Him [who hold Him in affectionate reverence, who obey Him, and who gratefully recognize the benefits that He has bestowed].
>
> 1 Corinthians 2:9

Dear reader, if you have made a recent decision to turn and follow Jesus, one of the very next things you need is to tell someone about that decision. Tell anyone; it doesn't matter; what matters is that you declare *with your mouth* what you have *decided in your heart*. This settles and ratifies your commitment. Next, ask *God* to guide you to a local Bible-believing church where you can fellowship with others of like mind and spirit. This will help you grow in your knowledge of *God* and acquire the *spiritual gifts* He has waiting for you (more on this in the pages to follow).

Now, some of you might *not* be able to immediately find and start attending a church. I usually steer away from television or online ministries because of the many that are misleading or even blatantly false. Recognizing false doctrine is something that usually comes to a believer over time. However, should you care to check out for yourself some ministries available over the airways, I will give you a short list of pastors and teachers who are genuinely anointed, teaching the Bible as the very *Word of God*, given through the *inspiration of Holy Spirit*. There are more than these with which I am familiar, but please ask *Holy Spirit* to guide you into all truth before listening to *any* pastor or teacher of *any* ministry. By asking for His guidance, *God* will certainly protect you from the *doctrines of demons.*

I have listed several ministries available over the airways or online with which I am familiar enough to recommend. You will find this list, as well as some Christian books that will help you grow in your knowledge of *God* and *His kingdom,* on page 108.

In the chapters to follow, you will find information and examples of how to conduct *effective* spiritual warfare against Satan and his legions.

- Praise and worship are indomitable weapons against the onslaught of the enemy (Isaiah 61, Joshua 6).
- There is the armor of God (Ephesians 6).
- Then we have the Blood of the Lamb (*Jesus*) and the word of our testimony (Revelation 12), which stand victorious against every obstacle that would challenge *God's* will for your life.

I hope that you will learn and proclaim *God's Word* and blessing over your life, family, and circumstances. The rewards are indescribable!

(See Numbers 6:24–26.)

I pray that you become familiar with the immense power of effective, regular prayer and how you can develop your own prayer life. My fervent prayer for you is that you will carefully and *sincerely* examine all areas of your life (including your private enjoyment of popular media), asking yourself the following question:

Are my days free from demonic and worldly influences? Am I certain? (Can we even pull that off in today's culture?) It is not a simple undertaking. I've found it *impossible* without directly including *Holy Spirit* in my efforts. As a prerequisite to having the Spirit's guidance, I must have a *daily intimate engagement in relationship with Jesus*, the One Who gave His all to save me. Here's how this works: I engage with *Father God through Jesus*, in prayer, study of His Word, and listening for and obeying *His still small voice*. But how easily we are drawn away by life's cares and enticements! It takes time to *sit in God's presence*, and from personal experience, I guarantee it won't happen with any consistency unless you purposefully schedule a time and place to get alone with *God*.

Jesus stole away with *His Father* in prayer before the rising of every sun. That is exactly how He received from the *Father* everything needed for that day, then again and again, throughout each day. Listen, if *Jesus* needed His alone time each morning with *the Father*, who am I to think that I can do just fine on my own? So many of us are so busy from the moment we wake up until our heads hit the pillow!

If you don't schedule a daily time to get alone with God, it won't happen.

Give God the first part of every day
before you get underway
and you will rarely have to say,
"Oh no! There I go again,
I went my own way,
(running amuck)
and going the wrong way."
Just consider the following:

The average American over the age of two spends more than thirty-four hours a week watching live television, says a new Nielsen report—plus another three to six hours watching taped programs…Children between two and eleven watch an average of twenty-four hours of TV a week, or three and a half hours a day.[1]

"Among smartphone users in the US, the time spent with their device is three hours, ten minutes per day."[2]

At a minimum, that equals one-quarter of an entire twenty-four-hour period spent with minds occupied on material such

---

1. *New York Daily News*, "Americans spend 34 hours a week watching TV, according to Nielsen numbers," last modified January 10, 2019, https://www.nydailynews.com/2012/09/19/americans-spend-34-hours-a-week-watching-tv-according-to-nielsen-numbers.
2. EMARKETER, "US Time Spent with Mobile 2019," last modified May 30, 2019, https://www.emarketer.com/content/us-time-spent-with-mobile-2019.

as breaking news reports, movies and shows with incredibly dark themes, YouTube, and popular media material, like Facebook and Twitter. The bulk of the materials coming across the airways and internet these days are a *far cry* from the kind of content useful to the building of *faith* and knowledge of *Jesus*, His Kingdom, and His will for our life! Our ears, eyes, and hearts turned toward *God and His soon-coming Kingdom*, the study of His Word, and prayer are indispensable in such a time as this! But our rapid rate of life and the lure of *many distractions* keep us from the very relief and protection afforded by a close and loving relationship with our *Creator*.

In Psalm 119:37, King David cries out to God, "Turn my eyes away from vanity [all those worldly, meaningless things that distract—let Your priorities be mine], And restore me [with renewed energy] in Your ways."

Being distracted from following the will of *God* is nothing new. Even mighty King David wrestled with sinful thoughts and desires presented on the stage of his life. *Had he remembered to ask God to keep his desires holy*, he probably would never have sinned with Bathsheba (a married neighbor *whose husband honorably served in David's army*). Bathsheba became pregnant with King David's baby. Furthermore, King David, after granting Bathsheba's husband a brief leave to visit his wife (hoping to blame the pregnancy on him), was then responsible for the husband's death by sending him to the front lines of the battlefield. *When facing temptation, do you have wisdom enough to ask the Lord to keep your desires holy?*

I pray that the message of this book serves to liberate your heart and mind from the ungodly influences of Satan and the smoke and mirrors of this corrupt worldly system! May you receive spiritual enlightenment guarding you and your family from the dark influence of Satan's schemes and this current *culture of lies*!

The Lord bless and keep you!

CHAPTER 3
Isn't the Bible Just Another Religious Book?

Now, some of my readers might be thinking, "That's all good for some people, but I've heard and read so many contradictory things about the Bible, I'm not even sure that it's true. How can I know?" *I'm glad you asked!*

Divinely Inspired?

Perhaps you are one of the many who grapple with the question of who is the source of what is written in the Bible. Is the Bible divinely inspired or just an ordinary religious book? What is distinctive about the Bible compared to all other books ever written? What evidence proves that the Bible is truly *God's divinely inspired Word?* Let's unpack this. There is no doubt that the Bible *claims* to be the *Word of God.*

> From childhood you have known the sacred writings (Hebrew Scriptures) which are able to give you the wisdom that leads to salvation through faith which is in Christ Jesus [surrendering your entire self to Him and having absolute confidence in His wisdom, power, and goodness]. All Scripture is God-breathed [*given by divine inspiration*] and is profitable for instruction, for conviction [of sin], for correction [of error and restoration to obedience], for training in righteousness.
>
> 2 Timothy 3:15–16 (emphasis added)

Down through history, *God* provided us with a roadmap. He foretold various signs and conditions through His prophets. These prophets spoke of things that [people] should watch for so that the *Messiah* [*Jesus Christ*] would be recognized and believed. These signs or prophecies were given to us in the Old Testament. The Old Testament is the part of the Bible written [long] before *Jesus* was born. Its writings were completed in 450 BC [before the birth of *Christ*]. The Old Testament, written *hundreds of years* before Jesus' birth, contains over three hundred prophecies that Christ fulfilled through His life, death, and resurrection.

Mathematically speaking, the odds of anyone fulfilling this amount of prophecy are staggering. Mathematicians put it this way:

One person fulfilling eight prophecies: 1 in 100,000,000,000,000,000.

One person fulfilling forty-eight prophecies: 1 chance in 10 to the 157th power.

One person fulfilling 300+ prophecies: Only Jesus![3]

Unlike prophecies found in other religious books or those given by men such as Nostradamus, biblical prophecies are highly detailed. Bear in mind that there are over *three hundred prophecies* in the Old Testament about *Jesus*. Not only was *Jesus'* lineage foretold, along with His locality of birth, but also that He would die by crucifixion and be raised to life again. Death by crucifixion didn't exist when the book of Isaiah was authored. But we see the *Savior, Jesus,* depicted as hanging on a tree in the Old Testament book of Isaiah, written about *seven hundred years before the birth of Christ Jesus.*

The Sin-Bearing Messiah

Who has believed our report?
And to whom has the arm of the Lord been revealed?
For He shall grow up before Him as a tender plant,
And as a root out of dry ground.
He has no form or comeliness;

---

3. CBN, "Biblical Prophecies Fulfilled by Jesus," last modified February 27, 2007, https://www2.cbn.com/article/prophecy/biblical-prophecies-fulfilled-jesus (emphasis added).

And when we see Him,
There is no beauty that we should desire Him.
He is despised and rejected by men,
A Man of sorrows and acquainted with grief.
And we hid, as it were, our faces from Him;
He was despised, and we did not esteem Him.
Surely He has borne our griefs
And carried our sorrows;
Yet we esteemed Him stricken,
Smitten by God, and afflicted.
But He was wounded for our transgressions,
He was bruised for our iniquities;
The chastisement for our peace was upon Him,
And by His stripes we are healed.
All we like sheep have gone astray;
We have turned, every one, to his own way;
And the Lord has laid on Him the iniquity of us all.
He was oppressed and He was afflicted,
Yet He opened not His mouth;
He was led as a lamb to the slaughter,
And as a sheep before its shearers is silent,
So He opened not His mouth.
He was taken from prison and from judgment,
And who will declare His generation?
For He was cut off from the land of the living;
For the transgressions of My people He was stricken.
And they made His grave with the wicked—
But with the rich at His death,
Because He had done no violence,
Nor was any deceit in His mouth.

> Isaiah 53:1–9 (NKJV)

The Bible has been repeatedly proven historically accurate. Through archeological and ancient manuscripts, evidence has been discovered and verified as authentic and has, in every instance, proven the validity of its writings throughout.

The book of John tells the [account] of *Jesus* restoring sight to a blind man by putting clay on his eyes and then having him wash it off with water from the [Pool of] Siloam…"Scholars have said that there wasn't a Pool of Siloam and that John was using a religious [metaphor to illustrate a point]," New Testament scholar James H. Charlesworth told the *Los Angeles Times*. "Now we have *found the Pool of Siloam*…exactly where John said it was…[the fourth book of the New Testament] is now shown to be grounded in history."

In 2004, workers attempting to repair a damaged sewer line discovered two steps leading to the pool. Archaeologists quickly took over and excavated the pool itself, which was a trapezoid about 69 meters (225 ft) long. They were also fortunate to find coins and pottery dating the pool to around the time of Jesus. In particular, four Alexander Jannaeus coins were buried in the plaster beneath the stone facade of the pool's steps. Jannaeus ruled Jerusalem from 103 BC to 76 BC, meaning that the pool was built no earlier than that time.

In a corner of the pool, archaeologists discovered roughly twelve more coins buried in silt. These coins were dated from AD 66 to AD 70, indicating that the pool was at least partially filled in by then. Together, the two groups of coins give us an estimate of how long the pool was used. A stone bottle cork and pottery shards also help to confirm the date.[4]

By providing us with the Bible, God demonstrates His love for us. Scriptures communicate to us what our *Creator* is like and how we can have a genuine relationship with Him. We could not have this guidance unless *God* had divinely revealed such things to us in the Bible. The Bible contains everything necessary for knowing God so that we might enjoy a true and joyful relationship with Him.

"For His divine power has bestowed on us [absolutely] everything necessary for [a dynamic spiritual] life and godliness,

---

4. Listverse, "10 Intriguing Pieces Of Evidence For Bible Stories," last modified July 28, 2015, https://listverse.com/2015/07/28/10-intriguing-pieces-of-evidence-for-bible-stories/.

through true and personal knowledge of Him who called us by His own glory and excellence" (2 Peter 1:3).

The contents of the Bible demonstrate that God wants a relationship with us, or He would not have provided specific guidelines on *how to* have a relationship with Him. The Bible's authority is distinct from that of any other book ever written. The demonstration of this power is seen in the countless lives that have been *supernaturally transformed*. Addicts, derelicts, deadbeats, prostitutes, hardened criminals, and even devotees of Satan; indeed, all types of sinners have already been liberated from the chains that bound them and kept them in darkness. And all this through the *good news* found in the pages of *God's Holy Word*. The Bible possesses a dynamic and transforming, supernatural power that is only feasible because it is *truly the Inspired Word of God (God-breathed)*!

> For the word of God is living and active and full of power [making it operative, energizing, and effective]. It is sharper than any two-edged sword, penetrating as far as the division of the soul and spirit [the completeness of a person], and of both joints and marrow [the deepest parts of our nature], exposing and judging the very thoughts and intentions of the heart.
>
> Hebrews 4:12

Even considering all the above information, some still argue that the Bible is unreliable simply because (as they claim) "truth is relative." Let's examine this questionable perception.

CHAPTER 4
Is Truth Relative?

Many are familiar with the idiom "Truth is relative" or the phrase "Perspective is everything." Rather than accepting these ideas at face value, let's discuss exactly where this train of thought could land you. First, consider the term "absolute truth," a fact that has been challenged by modern thinking with the idea that there *is no* absolute truth.

Let's use the effects of the laws of nature to refute this idea.
- The wind blows, moving things that were otherwise stationary.
- Refusing to accept this as an absolute truth could potentially put you in grave danger in the case of a tornado or hurricane.
- A crab digs a hole on the shoreline, and due to gravity, part of what he's trying to remove tumbles back down into his hole.
- You are fortunately *not* flying off the face of the earth into outer space due to gravity.
- The human body is composed of between 45 percent and 60 percent water, which you must constantly replenish.
- Refusing to accept this absolute truth will certainly be the death of you.

There are countless other potent examples of absolute truth, which we could spend hours discussing, but for now, the above examples have sufficed. Let's also unpeel the idea that truth is relative. First, ask yourself, "Relative to what? To what I believe?" If I make the statement that truth is relative, it really cannot be a fact *(if indeed truth is relative)* because the statement that truth is relative is also relative. This line of thinking is a perfect example of circular logic. Encyclopedia Britannica has the following to say about this type of logic: "A circular argument's premise explicitly or implicitly assumes that its conclusion is true rather than providing any supporting statements."

People often use the phrase "Truth is relative" when confronted with a believer in Jesus who starts to share with them the good news of salvation. A person might say something like, "God might be a reality for you, but to me, He doesn't exist."

This kind of statement is often touted as being open-minded and accepting, but in reality, it is judgmental and condescending, inferring that the speaker is correct and the person holding the belief in God is wrong. It is a veiled insult!

Now, let's examine the statement "Perception is everything." Here's what PhD Jim Taylor, a noted psychologist, has to say about this concept in an article written for *Psychology Today*:

> Let me state with an absolute sense of reality and without any perceptual flexibility at the outset that perception is NOT reality. As I am a word guy, meaning I believe that words powerfully shape our attitudes, beliefs, and, well, perceptions, let me start off by showing why perceptions and reality are different. Here is a dictionary definition of perception:
>
> - "The way of regarding, understanding, or interpreting something; a mental impression."
>
> And here is the dictionary definition of reality:
> - "The world or the state of things as they actually exist… existence that is absolute, self-sufficient, or objective, and not subject to human decisions or conventions."

Clearly, *perception* and *reality* have very different meanings. The former occurs entirely in the mind in which mental gymnastics can turn any belief into reality. The other exists completely outside of the mind and can't be easily manipulated.[5]

Further along in this article, the writer used mental illness as a solid example to demonstrate the difference between reality and perception. His illustration asks you to consider the perception of a person who is afflicted with a mental health issue such as Schizophrenia.

So, according to this article our perception will not necessarily always line up with facts. The example the writer used of mental health issues is a powerful example of the unreliability of this belief that perception is everything. Schizophrenia or severe manic-depressive episodes often dangerously alter a person's perception, diverting it far off the path of reality. We know that persons suffering from schizophrenic symptoms experience warped observations that can drive them even to murder those they *perceive* as some kind of threat. Those in the throes of a manic episode (perceiving that they have superpowers) have hurled themselves off of tall buildings (believing that they could fly), plummeting to their death.

It pays to exercise critical thinking when considering what we've heard or read from others. Truth is fact supported by evidence. If an idea or statement is not supported by verifiable evidence, then it must be relegated to the arena of *opinion*.

According to the Bible, truth is *an absolute*, and His name is Jesus. In speaking to His disciples regarding how they would know their way to where He was going after He left the earth, Jesus said, "I am the [only] Way [to God] and the [real] Truth and the [real] Life; no one comes to the Father but through Me" (John 14:6).

---

5. Jim Taylor, "Perception Is Not Reality," *Psychology Today*, August 5, 2019, https://www.psychologytoday.com/intl/blog/the-power-prime/201908/perception-is-not-reality.

Since we have already explored the validity of the Bible, let us remember that according to the Word of God, there *is objective, absolute truth*, but there is also a truth revealed in the Bible, referred to as *spiritual reality*. According to God's Word, spiritual reality is more of an objective truth than physical reality.

"So we look not at the things which are seen, but at the things which are unseen; for the things which are visible are temporal [just brief and fleeting], but the things which are invisible are *everlasting and imperishable*" (2 Corinthians 4:18; emphasis added).

The world we see is passing away. From cover to cover, multiple Bible passages discuss the spiritual realm in precise detail. The spiritual realm is not something ordinarily recognized on the physical plane of existence, but the Bible says that the *spiritual man* is capable of grasping and understanding *spiritual matters*. The Bible here, when referring to a *spiritual person*, is pointing to someone whose life is not controlled by fleshly and earthly desires but is led throughout their days by the Spirit of God. Here's what God's Word says about that.

> But the natural [unbelieving] man does not accept the things [the teachings and revelations] of the Spirit of God, for they are foolishness [absurd and illogical] to him; and he is incapable of understanding them, because they are spiritually discerned *and* appreciated, [and he is *unqualified to judge* spiritual matters].
>
> 1 Corinthians 2:14 (emphasis added)

"Spiritually discerned" means that it takes the supernatural power of God's Holy Spirit to obtain an understanding of spiritual matters that pertain to God. If you don't have God's Holy Spirit, He is available to you. However, you can't have Him unless you *want Jesus as Lord* because Jesus is the One Who sends Holy Spirit to live inside of you.

"When the Advocate comes, *whom I will send to you from the Father*—the Spirit of truth who proceeds from the Father—He will testify about Me" (John 15:26, BSB; emphasis added).

"And in Him, having heard and believed the word of truth—the gospel of your salvation—you were sealed with the promised Holy Spirit" (Ephesians 1:13, BSB).

To sum this up, if you have confessed and turned away from your sinful ways and are convinced that you need the Savior, Jesus, and *in your heart hold a true desire for Him to be Lord of your whole life, then the Spirit of God lives inside of your person.* You will be aware of God's presence because Holy Spirit will *assure you* (bear witness with your spirit) that you belong to Jesus.

"The Spirit Himself bears witness with our spirit that we are children of God" (Romans 8:16, BLB).

If you are living without the Spirit of God guiding and protecting your way, you have left yourself open to strong delusion. Delusion is a lie that you embrace that obstructs your capacity to see and act upon reality. According to the Bible, delusion is the result of *persistently rejecting the truth.*

> The coming of the lawless one will be accompanied by the working of Satan, with every kind of power, sign, and false wonder, and with every *wicked deception* directed against those who are perishing, *because they refused the love of the truth* that would have saved them. For this reason God will send them a *powerful delusion* so that they believe the lie, in order that judgment may come upon all who have disbelieved the truth *and delighted in wickedness.*
>
> 2 Thessalonians 2:9–12 (BSB; emphasis added)

Dear reader, please note in this verse above that those upon whom God sends strong delusion had *already refused* to accept the truth about Him, and furthermore, these are those who have *taken delight in wickedness.* God is gracious and kind, offering the truth of His redemptive power through Jesus Christ to the entire world. This verse is talking about those who have refused God's truth and salvation, preferring to walk in their wicked ways, apart from God.

That is why I am asking you to consider whether perhaps the real reason behind your doubt is based on your hopes of not admitting your sin to God. In other words, are you trying to convince yourself (with all the fanciful arguments) that you need not give account to your Creator for your actions because He may not even exist? In your own perception, are you deluding yourself into believing that everything is okay with you?

Please listen. If God's Spirit does not bear witness with your spirit that you are His, you may not belong to Him. You might already know that you don't belong to Jesus, or you might have assumed that you are a Christian because you were born into a Christian family or because you are a member of a certain church or pursue other Christian activities. Dear ones, we are in the last hours of the last days. *Don't reject the truth.* If you don't have certainty, *don't stop seeking God* until *you know that you know* that He is yours, and you are His. When time is no more, this is the *only truth that matters*!

CHAPTER 5
Let's Take a Look at the Occult

Did God Really Say…?

Merriam-Webster's Dictionary says that "deceit" is "the act of causing someone to accept as true or valid what is false or invalid."[6]

In her online article, "Fair Is Foul and Foul Is Fair: Witchcraft and Deception," Cyndi Brannen, a practicing witch, says,

> Perhaps the founders of the modern witchcraft revolution themselves were engaging in deception in their careful use of certain terms, including *Wicca, to describe witchcraft in ways that are more socially acceptable.*
>
> No wonder given the long history of persecution that our ancestors endured. Witches have always been part of society, often both reviled and valued, but *always seen as deceivers.*
>
> *Witchcraft and deception are deeply interwoven,* from the lies told about us to our own need to self-protect by concealing our identity.
>
> When it comes to practicing witchcraft, our work often includes forms of deception, ranging from the methods we use *to practicing them on others without consent.*[7]

---

6. *Merriam-Webster.com Dictionary*, "Deceit Definition & Meaning," accessed April 10, 2024, https://www.merriam-webster.com/dictionary/deceit.
7. Patheos, "Fair Is Foul and Foul Is Fair: Witchcraft and Deception," last modified June 11, 2020, https://www.patheos.com/blogs/keepingherkeys/2019/10/witchcraft-and-deception (emphasis added).

CHAPTER 6
The Kingdom of Satan

When *Jesus* spoke of Satan, He called him the father of lies. Jesus said, "When he [Satan] speaks a falsehood, he speaks what is natural to him, for he is a liar [himself] and the father of lies and of all that is false" (John 8:44).

The first recorded lie was chronicled in Genesis 3:1–5 (emphasis added):

> Now the serpent was more crafty (subtle, skilled in deceit) than any living creature of the field which the Lord God had made. And the serpent (Satan) said to the woman, "*Can it really be* that God has said, 'You shall not eat from any tree of the garden'?" And the woman said to the serpent, "We may eat fruit from the trees of the garden, except the fruit from the tree which is in the middle of the garden. God said, 'You shall not eat from it nor touch it, otherwise you will die.'" But the serpent said to the woman, "You certainly will not die! For God knows that on the day you eat from it your eyes will be opened [that is, you will have greater awareness], and you will *be like God*, knowing [the difference between] good and evil."

Notice Satan's crafty suggestion, "*Can it really be* that God has said," insinuating that our Creator is a liar, which is the first and *greatest* recorded lie in all of history.

Adam and, subsequently, Eve were placed in the pristine garden by God. Before their disobedience, the first man and woman enjoyed a regular, intimate, and wonderful friendship with their *Creator*. They adored mornings, walking with their *Creator* through the garden in the cool of the day. They communicated one-on-one with Him, basking in the light of His glory. The Bible doesn't indicate how long this ideal relationship lasted before *the father of lies* stepped into the picture.

From the beginning, Satan has been a liar, convincing millions that they, too, can "*be like God*" or become gods themselves. The devil lied to Eve to lure her away from the loving relationship she and Adam enjoyed with their *Creator*. The tragic result of our first ancestors' disobedience was the loss of *connection and intimacy* with God. This was *spiritual death* and is what our Creator referred to when warning Adam that he would surely die should he eat of the Tree of the Knowledge of Good and Evil. What was once a joyous relationship was now ripped apart by the sin of doubting God's goodness, by doubting God's love; and not trusting His intentions toward us. When sin entered the world, shame alighted, causing Adam and Eve to desperately attempt to hide themselves from God. Shame *always* compels people to hide from God. It's a futile undertaking. *God is everywhere all at once!*

"Where can I go from Your Spirit? Or where can I flee from Your presence? If I ascend to heaven, You are there; If I make my bed in Sheol (the nether world, the place of the dead), behold, You are there" (Psalm 139:7–8).

Because *God* is pure and holy, sin can't be in or even approach His presence. Therefore, a great chasm of separation from our Creator was incited by Adam and Eve's sin. Not the sin of biting into an apple or any other fruit, but the sin of listening to Satan's bidding rather than trusting and following what *God* had spoken to them. The earth also fell into the hands of Satan, thereby plunging into decay. Instead of walking with God, we have tumbled from our position as *God's* stewards of the earth, and Satan now holds the whole planet under his influence.

"We know [for a fact] that we are of God, and the whole world [around us] lies in the power of the evil one [opposing God and His precepts]" (1 John 5:19).

Earth was originally established by God as a "colony" of His Heavenly Kingdom. God established the whole earth under the care and charge of those who were created in His image, namely, we humans. Our primary purpose was to have an *intimate relationship with our Creator and carry out His perfect will here on earth* through devout stewardship of His creation (the earth and all its creatures).

> Then God said, "Let Us (Father, Son, Holy Spirit) make man in Our image, according to Our likeness [not physical, but a spiritual personality and moral likeness]; and let them *have complete authority* over the fish of the sea, the birds of the air, the cattle, and over the entire earth, and over everything that creeps and crawls on the earth."
>
> Genesis 1:26 (emphasis added)

As part of our very nature, we were created to govern through oversight. We lost our right to preside over God's creation by doubting His *truth, faithfulness, perfection, holiness, and good intentions* toward us. Our ancestor's faith in God was usurped by transferring that faith onto the created rather than the Creator. *Through this shift in the object of our faith and trust, we lost our access to intimate fellowship with our Creator.*

Instead of keeping focus on the Word God had given to them, they chose to believe the lie of Satan, who hates *God*, despises *God's children*, and instead wants to set *himself* up as god! Our rebellion and fall from God's original design and perfect will for us created a chasm between people and God. (Sin cannot stand in the presence of a perfect, holy God). This immense chasm of separation from our Creator and loss of control over ourselves and our environment is the very core of our angst and longing. This yearning to regain control is common to every soul, compelling each one on a seemingly endless pursuit of something bigger and more powerful than us. The question of who we are and why we exist skulks in the back of every inquiring mind. This anguish motivates us to search for answers and purpose that are only discovered in a loving, intimate relationship with *our very source*, our *Creator*, *God*, through His Son, *Jesus*.

The occult is intricately interwoven with deceit and the exercise of power and control. I suggest that here in the garden (with Satan as the villain), this account of our falling out of the relationship with God is where we find the birthing of the occult into the World. Satan has been trying to sell the lie that we can achieve godhead ever since he tried to claim it as his own!

"I will ascend above the heights of the clouds; I will make myself like the Most High" (Isaiah 14:14).

Satan, originally created as one of God's mightiest and profoundly beautiful angels, named Lucifer, presided over one-third of Heaven's lower-ranked angels. He became inflamed with pride over his beauty and strength, thinking that he could rise up in his own power and become like God. He was judged and evicted from Heaven for his rebellion, manipulating those lower angels that were in his charge into following him in his insurrection.

For a brilliant and detailed teaching on this scriptural account of Satan's origin, YouTube has videos of Derek Prince's teachings. Look up his three-part series called "The Enemies We Face" and listen closely to part one. I encourage you to also make time to listen to and absorb the entire series, as it reveals quite a bit regarding witchcraft and touches on information about the antichrist.

The underlying appeal of various Occult rituals or practices is the aim of achieving "godhead," or *power over one's environment and other people*. It is at the core of all *manipulation* of the natural and supernatural realm.

CHAPTER 7
A Brief Overview of the Occult in the Bible

Let's take a brief excursion through the biblical records of the occult. Before beginning the writing of this book, I poured many hours of research into the occult. I researched many religious practices and beliefs throughout history and across the globe. It was incredibly extensive. Because of that, and for the sake of simplicity, this section will focus only on Occult practices found in the Old Testament of the Bible. Then, I will discuss the power (kingdom) behind those practices and how the same power is currently abundantly active as the "hidden" source of all cultural and sociological upheaval throughout the United States (and elsewhere).

As for the rest of my occult research, you will find it in the back of this book. What you will find are my notes recorded as I conducted my research. Some results come from written works or interviews, which are reliable resources. However, the bulk of the material was found online. Therefore, I cannot vouch for the reliability of all of it. Researching this subject matter will take one down all kinds of frightening, dark paths on which I did not care to linger! If you care to look through these pages (118-141), this material will reveal details of societies practicing and participating in magic, sorcery, and deity worship (some of which require human sacrifice, cannibalism, and other unnerving occult activities). The information is included for those who have only a general idea of such things. It is a synopsis and by no means thorough. I've become convinced that it is absolutely essential to raise awareness as to the immensity of Satan's kingdom and its supernatural influence on today's governments and society.

If you already have spiritual revelation as to the danger of occult activity, you may choose not to read it. However, if you read it, perhaps you will recognize similarities of beliefs and rituals across the globe and throughout time. While doing this research, I became keenly aware of a global theme common to all practices of the occult, and I could not help but come to the conclusion that it is all assembled and fueled by the kingdom of Satan.

The occult is a universal phenomenon. Every society, every age has carried some system of supernatural belief. In every civilization, there have been those who harness or manipulate supernatural powers. Even today, magic infiltrates our lives; some have charms worn on the body to bring luck during exams or interviews, and others nod at lone magpies to ward off bad luck. People avoid breaking a mirror or crossing paths with a black cat. Iceland has *an elf whisperer* who claims the ability to see, speak to, and negotiate with supernatural creatures still believed to live in Iceland's wilderness.[8]

President Ronald Reagan's wife regularly consulted with her astrological advisor, Joan Quigley, while former President Reagan was in office. Quigley later wrote the following in a book regarding her relationship with the Reagans, titled *What Does Joan Say?* "Not since the days of the Roman emperors, and never in the history of the United States presidency, has an astrologer played such a significant role in the nation's affairs of State."

All of this, taken together, speaks to me absolutely of just one source that perpetuates these practices throughout the world. The Bible says that the source is Satan, the *deceiver of the whole world!*

---

8. Allison D. Reid, "Medieval Monday: The Service of Magic," accessed July 9, 2024, https://allisondreid.com/2019/10/28/medieval-monday-the-service-of-magic.

> The growing interest in the occult is a phenomenon of our times. Some of the more benign but still dangerous [forms] are astrology and fortunetelling.
>
> These practices may seem innocent to the majority of people, but they are doors to a world that, once opened, are difficult to close. Some occult practices can be attributed to quackery and illusion. However, it would be biblically irresponsible not to recognize that the world of the occult is ultimately controlled and empowered by Satan and his demonic legions.
>
> Most practitioners of the occult see little cause for alarm in their pursuits. In reality, this thinking is very naïve. The many forms of the occult can lead people into spiritual bondage.[9]

Intense fascination with the occult in modern society has recently exploded, expanding rapidly.

As a verb, the word "occult" simply means "to cover," implying something has been hidden. Occultic concepts pertaining to the esoteric are *hidden things or phenomena* that (under normal circumstances) are undetectable. There is a huge list of rituals and concepts that fall within the parameters of occultic practices, encompassing a wide range of beliefs. Some of the more commonly known include astrology (horoscopes), psychic abilities and implements (fortune telling, tarot cards, Ouija boards, etc.), extra sensory perception, witchcraft, Wicca, paganism, channeling, transcendental meditation, deity worship, and numerous others that are discussed in more detail in the final chapter of this book.

Experimentation with or practicing occultic activities invites Satan. Be certain that he will RSVP you with a resounding "Yes"! As he and his evil cohorts invade your personal territory and your mind you can become so saturated with his darkness that you lose your sense of reality. Involvement in the occult may even drive you to suicide.

---

9. Apocalypse soon, "Divine Condemnation of the Occult," accessed July 9, 2024, https://apocalypsesoon.org/x-file-34.

When Jesus encountered a father whose son was demonized, Jesus asked for more information. The boy's father told Jesus of the young man's repeated attempts at suicide.

> Jesus asked the boy's father, "How long has this been with him?"
>
> "From childhood," he said. "It often throws him into the fire or into the water, trying to kill him. But if You can do anything, have compassion on us and help us."
>
> He [Jesus] rebuked the unclean spirit. "You deaf and mute spirit," He said, "I command you to come out and never enter him again."
>
> Mark 9:21–22, 25b (BSB)

Occultic practices originate and are sustained through the kingdom of Satan and his demonic forces. For those practicing its arts, *the gateways* through which they (the keepers of darkness) manifest and infiltrate are burst open as an inevitable, implacable, invisible presence swarms into their lives.

Only the more superior power of the Lord Jesus Christ can evict these squatters and seal shut the portals through which they flew!

Scripture records dire warnings against the occult, spoken by God to individuals and nations. He gave specific instructions to the Israelites as they were ready to inhabit the land to which He led them.

> When you enter the land which the LORD your God is giving you, you shall not learn to imitate the detestable (repulsive) practices of those nations. There shall not be found among you anyone who makes his son or daughter pass through the fire [as a sacrifice], one who uses divination *and* fortune-telling, one who practices witchcraft, or one who interprets omens, or a sorcerer, or one who casts a charm *or* spell, or a medium, or a spiritist, or a necromancer [who seeks the dead]. For everyone who does these things is utterly repulsive to the LORD; and because of these detestable practices the LORD your God is driving them out before you. You shall be blameless (complete, perfect) before the LORD your God.

> For these nations which you shall dispossess listen to those who practice witchcraft and to diviners *and* fortune-tellers, but as for you, the LORD your God has not allowed you to do so.
>
> Deuteronomy 18:9–14

There is much to consider when deciphering why God's people repeatedly turned away from God in worship of false gods. There is a spirit of bondage that accompanied them when they left the captivity of the Egyptian Empire. Egypt is where they were enslaved (in bondage) for over four hundred years. While in captivity, they were surrounded by a society steeped in occultic practices. Long after they escaped from Egyptian bondage, they remained in the mindset of a slave. This opened the way for Satan to keep them in bondage to idolatrous religions.

The Occult in the Old Testament

> God pronounced severe judgment on the people of Judah and Jerusalem because they worshiped "the queen of heaven" (Jeremiah 7:17–20, 44:15–19).
>
> As early as the twenty-fifth century BC, people of Ur of the Chaldees in Sumeria worshiped a mother-goddess named *Ishtar*. Around the same time the Minoans of Crete [venerated] a mother-goddess…Later, the people of Cyprus revered a *goddess patterned after the Sumerian Ishtar* and [afterward embraced] by the Greeks as Aphrodite, or Astarte.
>
> The Babylonians…around the twenty-second century BC, [focused their spiritual] beliefs to the heavenly bodies. They [took] the planets as [their] gods and goddesses, *[endowing] the planet Venus with the [spirit of] Ishtar.*
>
> The Babylonians worshiped *Ishtar* as "The Virgin," "The Holy Virgin," "The Virgin Mother," "Goddess of Goddesses," and "*Queen of Heaven* and Earth." They exclaimed, "Ishtar is great! Ishtar is Queen! My Lady is exalted, my Lady is Queen… There is none like unto her." *[They assigned her miraculous powers, such as healing the sick and raising the dead.]*

In Babylonian mythology *Ishtar* wore a crown and was related to Tammuz, who sometimes was portrayed as her son and other times as her lover.

> The *Sumerian-Babylonian Ishtar was the [complement] of the Egyptian Isis and the [archetype of] Grecian Aphrodite, Roman Venus, Assyrian Nina, Phrygian and Roman Cybele, Phoenician Astarte, and Astarte of Syria. In essence they were the same mother-goddess.*

The Egyptians called Isis "the Great Mother" and "the Mother of God." Isis worship spread to Italy by the second century and then throughout the entire Roman Empire.

The people of Phoenicia worshiped *Baal*. Baalism included the worship of *Molech* with *fiery sacrifices of children* and the worship of Astarte, the Phoenician Ishtar *Queen of Heaven*.

When the Phoenician princess *Jezebel* became the wife of King *Ahab* of the northern Kingdom of Israel, she [manipulated] him to fully establish *Baal* worship in his realm (1 Kings 16:29–33, 21:25–26). This move entangled the people of Israel in Queen-of-Heaven worship. As a result, God judged them with the Assyrian Captivity (2 Kings 17:5–7, 16–18).

Athaliah, daughter of Ahab and Jezebel, became the wife of King Jehoram of the Kingdom of Judah. She influenced him to do what her father had done—fully establish Baal worship in his kingdom (2 Kings 8:16–18). Her son, Ahaziah, the next king of Judah, did the same (2 Kings 8:25–27), as did King Manasseh (2 Kings 21:1–6). These actions would have entangled the people of Judah in Queen-of-Heaven worship. Thus God judged them with the Babylonian Captivity (2 Kings 21:12–14).[10]

In spite of God's numerous prophetic warnings, Israel often turned their back on the blessings of their relationship with God.

"For My people have committed two evils: They have abandoned (rejected) Me, The fountain of living water, And they have

---

10. Israel My Glory, "The 'Queen of Heaven,'" last modified August, 2004, https://israelmyglory.org/article/the-queen-of-heaven.

carved out their own cisterns, Broken cisterns That cannot hold water" (Jeremiah 2:13).

In the book of Amos, we read of God's judgement on Israel (because of their occultic practices) resulting in their captivity. "But ye have borne the tabernacle of your *Moloch* and *Chiun* your images, the star of your god, which ye made to yourselves. Therefore will I cause you to go into captivity beyond Damascus, saith the Lord, whose name is The God of hosts" (Amos 5:26–27, KJV; emphasis added).

There are numerous references in the Old Testament describing to what depths of evil the Israelites fell by adopting the gods and goddesses of the surrounding pagan nations.

God's people refused direct warnings from the prophets and blatantly said *no* to the Word of the Lord!

> Then all the men who knew that their wives were burning incense to other gods, and all the women standing by—a great assembly—along with all the people living in the land of Egypt and in Pathros said to Jeremiah, "As for the word you have spoken to us in the name of the LORD, *we will not listen to you*! Instead, we will do everything we vowed to do: We will burn incense to the *Queen of Heaven* and offer drink offerings to her, just as we, our fathers, our kings, and our officials did in the cities of Judah and in the streets of Jerusalem."
>
> Jeremiah 44:15–17 (BSB; emphasis added)

> They abandoned all the commandments of the Lord their God and made for themselves cast images of two calves; and they made an Asherah [idol] and worshiped all the [starry] host of heaven and served Baal. *They made their sons and their daughters pass through the fire [as human sacrifices], and* used divination [to foretell the future] and enchantments; and they sold themselves to do evil in the sight of the Lord, provoking Him to anger. Therefore the Lord was very angry with Israel and removed them from His sight; none [of the tribes] was left except the tribe of Judah.
>
> 2 Kings 17:16–18 (emphasis added)

Sadly, only a few kings found in the Old Testament stood against the idolatry of the nation of Israel, destroying the High Places, Asherim, and Idols of the false gods in the Holy Land. *Asa, Jehoshaphat, Hezekiah, and Josiah* were loyal to God and ordered their destruction (though some were more thorough than others in this task). Most notable of these kings is Josiah, who was the only king who followed after the Lord all the days of his life.

> So the king stood by the pillar and made a covenant before the LORD to follow the LORD and to keep His commandments, decrees, and statutes with all his heart and all his soul, and to carry out the words of this covenant that were written in this book. And all the people entered into the covenant.
>
> 2 Kings 23:3 (BSB)

> Then the king commanded Hilkiah the high priest and the priests of the second rank and the doorkeepers to bring out of the temple of the Lord all the *articles made for Baal, for [the goddess] Asherah, and for all the [starry] host of heaven*; and he burned them outside Jerusalem in the fields of the Kidron, and carried their ashes to Bethel [where Israel's idolatry began]. He got rid of the idolatrous *priests whom the kings of Judah had ordained to burn incense [to pagan gods]* in the high places in Judah's cities and all around Jerusalem—also those who *burned incense to Baal, to the sun, to the moon, to the constellations [of the zodiac], and to all the [starry] host of heaven.* Josiah brought out the Asherah from the house of the Lord to the Brook Kidron outside Jerusalem, and burned it there, and ground it to dust, and threw its dust on the graves of the common people [who had sacrificed to it]. And he *tore down the houses of the [male] cult prostitutes, which were at the house (temple) of the Lord, where the women were weaving [tent] hangings for the Asherah [shrines].* Then Josiah brought all the [idolatrous] priests from the cities of Judah, and desecrated the *high places where the priests had burned incense [to idols],* from Geba to Beersheba, [that is, north to south]; and he tore down the high places of the gates which were at the entrance of the gate of Joshua the governor of the city, which were on

one's left at the city gate. However, the priests of the high places were not allowed to go up to the altar of the Lord in Jerusalem [to serve], but they ate unleavened bread among their brothers. *Josiah also defiled Topheth, which is in the Valley of Ben-hinnom (son of Hinnom), so that no man could make his son or his daughter pass through the fire [as a burnt offering] for Molech*. And he got rid of the horses that the kings of Judah had given [in worship] to the sun at the entrance of the house of the Lord, by the chamber of Nathan-melech the official, which was in the annex; *and he burned the chariots of the sun. The altars [dedicated to the starry host of heaven] which were on the roof*, the upper chamber of Ahaz, which the kings of Judah had made, and the altars which Manasseh had made in the two courtyards of the house of the Lord, the king tore down; and he smashed them there and threw their dust into the Brook Kidron. The king *desecrated the high places* which were opposite [east of] Jerusalem, which were on the right (south) of *the mount of corruption which Solomon the king of Israel had built for Ashtoreth* the repulsiveness of the Sidonians, for Chemosh the repulsiveness of Moab, and for Milcom the repulsiveness of the sons (descendants) of Ammon. *He broke in pieces the sacred pillars (cultic memorial stones*, images) and cut down the Asherim and replaced them with human bones [to desecrate the places forever].

2 Kings 23:4–14 (emphasis added)

God promised to drive out from before the Israelites those who occupied the promised land that they were about to enter. These were pagan nations, steeped in the practice of sacrifice of their children to fire, divination, witchcraft, sorcery, deity worship, and so on.

The Bible is clear in its condemnation of these practices.

When you enter the land which the Lord your God is giving you, you shall not learn to imitate the detestable (repulsive) practices of those nations. There shall not be found among you anyone who makes his son or daughter pass through the fire [as a sacrifice], one who uses divination and fortune-telling, one who practices witchcraft, or one who interprets omens, or a sorcerer, or one who casts a charm or spell, or a medium, or a spiritist, or a necromancer [who seeks the dead]. *For everyone who does these things is utterly repulsive to the Lord*; and because of these detestable practices the Lord your God is driving them out before you.

Deuteronomy 18:9–12 (emphasis added)

In spite of God's dire warning, His people worshiped the main deities of the surrounding pagan nations. There were others, but the three major players were *Baal, Ishtar* and *Molech*.

Baal was the dominant god of the Canaanite Pantheon. His name means "lord."

Baal was associated with fertility, steering Israel into the worship of nature. In biblical cultures, nearly all common people were completely reliant on nature to supply their daily sustenance (crops and livestock, fishing). The flourishing of these sources of sustenance was of *chief concern*. In today's world, we also focus on the acquisition of provisions and belongings. We replace the concern for healthy crops and livestock with concern for the flourishing of our bank accounts and the prestige of ownership. In other words, the worship of money.

"As for the rich in this present world, instruct them not to be conceited and arrogant, nor to set their hope on the uncertainty of riches, but on God, who richly and ceaselessly provides us with everything for our enjoyment" (1 Timothy 6:17).

Instead of the Creator, people worship the created.

For the wrath of God is revealed from heaven against all ungodliness and unrighteousness of people who suppress the truth in unrighteousness, because that which is known about God is evident within them; for God made it evident to them. For since the creation of the world His invisible attributes, that is, His eternal power and divine nature, have been clearly perceived, being understood by what has been made, so that they are without excuse. For even though they knew God, they did not honor Him as God or give thanks, but they became futile in their reasonings, and their senseless hearts were darkened. Claiming to be wise, they became fools, and they exchanged the glory of the incorruptible God for an image in the form of corruptible mankind, of birds, four-footed animals, and crawling creatures.

Therefore God gave them up to vile impurity in the lusts of their hearts, so that their bodies would be dishonored among them. For they exchanged the truth of God for falsehood, and worshiped and served the creature rather than the Creator, who is blessed forever. Amen.

Romans 1:18–25 (NASB)

Molech

According to biblical accounts, King Solomon was responsible for introducing the worship of Molech to the people of Israel.

For when Solomon was old, his wives turned his heart away after other gods; and his heart was not completely devoted to the Lord his God, as was the heart of his father David. For Solomon went after Ashtoreth, the [fertility] goddess of the Sidonians, and after Milcom the horror (detestable idol) of the Ammonites. Solomon did evil [things] in the sight of the Lord, and did not follow the Lord fully, as his father David had done. Then Solomon built a high place for [worshiping] Chemosh the horror (detestable idol) of Moab, on the hill which is east of Jerusalem, and for *Molech* the horror (detestable idol) of the sons of Ammon. And he did the same for all of his foreign wives, who burned incense and sacrificed to their gods.

1 Kings 11:4–8

"Molech" is sometimes spelled "Moloch," *and there are other variations of the name.* Moloch was also associated with Baal and was the demonic god who received human sacrifice (mostly of children), apparently as penance for sinful acts and to restore favor. The idol Molech is a huge image of a bull with outstretched arms (to receive its host) and a furnace for a belly. Babies were placed on a slanted platform at the top of the beast's belly, allowing each victim to roll down into the blazing belly of the idol. During these ceremonies, deafening drumming and music mesmerized the attendees and drowned out the gut-wrenching screams of burning babies. These atrocious sacrifices were offered to Molech in hopes that he would *grant well-being* to the devotee.

Today, babies are sacrificed on the altar of self-indulgence at abortion clinics (erected and sustained by the *spirit of Molech*). The reasons women seek abortions are varied, but they all boil down to *promoting the well-being* of the expectant mother at the cost of the baby's life. Do you recognize the motive as the same as those during the sacrificing of babies and children to *Molech*? Since its legalization in the early '70s, in the USA alone, more than 63,459,781 babies have lost their lives to abortion (National Right to Life Association, published 2021).

I am also convinced that the *spirit of Molech and Ishtar* are fueling childhood sex trafficking. No one has even the slightest idea as to the number of little ones whose lives have been ripped to shreds or chemically burned to death, sacrificed on the brazen altars of *Molech* and *Ishtar*.

God help us!

Ishtar

In ancient Mesopotamia, the priests and priestesses of the popular goddess <u>Inanna</u> (*better known as <u>Ishtar</u>*) were *bisexual and transgender*. One of the aspects of the goddess considered most awe-inspiring was *her ability to turn men into women and women into men,* the power of transformation.[11]

Ishtar was worshiped by ancient Israelites as the queen of Heaven (Jeremiah 44:19) and was also known for her *houses of the male cult prostitutes* (2 Kings 23:29).

Inanna is the ancient Sumerian goddess of love, sensuality, fertility, procreation, and also of war. She later became identified by the Akkadians and Assyrians as the goddess Ishtar, and further with the Hittite Sauska, the Phoenician Astarte and the Greek Aphrodite, among many others.[12]

The Spirit of Ishtar in the United States

In 2021, about 42,000 children and teens across the United States received a diagnosis of gender dysphoria, nearly triple the number in 2017, according to data Komodo [Health] compiled for Reuters. Gender dysphoria is defined as the distress caused by a discrepancy between a person's gender identity and the one assigned to them at birth.

Overall, the analysis found that at least 121,882 children ages 6 to 17 were diagnosed with gender dysphoria from 2017 through 2021.

Over the last five years, there were at least 4,780 adolescents who started on puberty blockers and had a prior gender dysphoria diagnosis.

---

11. World History Encyclopedia, "LGBTQ+ in the Ancient World," last modified June 25, 2021, https://www.worldhistory.org/article/1790/lgbtq-in-the-ancient-world (emphasis added).
12. World History Encyclopedia, "Inanna," last modified October 15, 2010, https://www.worldhistory.org/Inanna.

By suppressing sex hormones, puberty-blocking medications stop the onset of secondary sex characteristics, such as breast development and menstruation in adolescents assigned female at birth. For those assigned male at birth, the drugs inhibit development of a deeper voice and an Adam's apple and growth of facial and body hair. They also limit growth of genitalia.

The Komodo analysis of insurance claims found 56 genital surgeries among patients ages 13 to 17 with a prior gender dysphoria diagnosis from 2019 to 2021.[13]

Until the 1960s, alternate sexual orientation was something consigned to secrecy. But, about the same time that the *Judeo-Christian God* was kicked out of our schools and public forums, a push toward normalizing these sexual lifestyles began. The campaign continued, growing in number and strength with each passing year, finally bursting into mainstream society as a great water balloon dropped from the sky.

The sexual revolution of the '60s and '70s was founded by *the spirit of Ishtar* and served as a jumping-off platform on which acceptance of homosexuality, transgenderism, and all such sexual deviation was launched. Today, this lifestyle is celebrated all the way up through the Whitehouse, being flaunted across all forms of media, advertisements, and entertainment, and is proudly displayed as a flag on the lawn of the forty-sixth President.

At this point, you might ask why I would focus on these specific demonic gods and the mechanisms of today's US cultural and spiritual upheaval. I'm actually not comparing them… *they are the same spirit beings*, having returned from their wandering through dry places and emerging from behind the secrecy of Freemasonry.

---

13. Robin Respaut and Chad Terhune, "Putting numbers on the rise in children seeking gender care," *Reuters*, October 6, 2022, https://www.reuters.com/investigates/special-report/usa-transyouth-data.

The secret society of Freemasons established the street design, architecture and monuments of Washington DC (designed by Pierre L'Enfant) to reflect the carefully guarded beliefs of Masons. Spirits of ancient gods and goddesses, having taken refuge in the darkness of Masonic rituals, were awaiting the New Age and their release from secrecy.

> Washington DC has been mapped as an earthly reflection of the celestial canopy above, designed with over thirty different zodiacs matching the constellations in the sky. In the National Academy of Sciences, twelve of the zodiacs are displayed in relief on the metal doors of the building. The Federal Reserve Board Building adds an additional two zodiacs designed in glass which glow with light. The Library of Congress Building displays another five zodiacs, as do many other important buildings in Washington DC.[14]

These ancient demonic gods gained their point of entry through broken-down borders of God's protection over the United States. Spiritual bulwarks, formed by ranks of holy angels. The angel armies of God were withdrawn as the United States fell from God's favor, turning our backs on long-held, sacred beliefs, abandoning the homeland to the doctrine of demons and the idolatry of self-indulgence. These foul supernatural beings have been waiting on the "back burner" of humanity since the huge expansion of Christianity evicted them from mainstream society during the reign of Constantine.

The disciple of Jesus, Peter, first introduced Christianity to Rome. Over time, Christianity and faith grew in numbers and power. In 313 AD, Emperor Constantine issued the *Edict of Milan*, which accepted Christianity and later became the official religion of the Roman Empire. From this point forward, veneration of

---

14. The Masonic Philosophical Society, "How did Freemasonry Influence the Design of Washington, D.C.?" last modified November 29, 2019, https://blog.philosophicalsociety.org/2019/11/29/freemasonry-design-washington-dc.

various gods and goddesses fell out of practice, thus greatly reducing their demonic influence and, therefore, power over much of the world. Human sacrifice and similarly vile practices gradually declined, remaining in only pockets of society.

Individuals and the Occult

Personal involvement in occultic practices is a slippery path that is now easily accessed (even by our children). The internet has become a portal to specific information and even membership into a myriad of occultic ideologies. While the benefits are highly touted, the underlying driving force is ordinarily *occulted* (hidden) from the seeker. Demonic oppression, bondage, and for some, even possession will be the final outcome of entering into this realm. The Bible says that those who practice such things are accursed. "Accursed" means "to be *under a curse*." God warned the Israelites in Deuteronomy against allowing any such things into their homes. God has not changed His mind; there remains a curse on such things and everyone who is involved.

"And you must not bring any detestable thing into your house, *or you, like it,* will be set apart for destruction. You are to utterly detest and abhor it, because it is *set apart for destruction*" (Deuteronomy 7:26, BSB; emphasis added).

It is not to the Jews only, nor is this pronouncement found only in the Old Testament. The book of Revelation explicitly lists these practices as an abomination, which means to be accursed. Moreover, you would also be eternally excluded from God's Kingdom if you do not repent and continue with such things.

How much more of a dire warning can I give you?

In the verse below, Jesus is speaking, and He is referring to those who will not be entering into His Kingdom.

"But outside are the dogs, the *sorcerers*, the sexually immoral, the murderers, the idolaters, and everyone who loves and practices falsehood" (Revelation 22:15, BSB; emphasis added).

What about your *here and now?* The above-mentioned consequences of this pathway are eternal, but involvement will also ultimately wreak havoc on you in the land of the living. Demonic powers that invade you as you become more entrenched in these ideologies are ultimately seeking your destruction. Many become deluded and are driven to madness or even to suicide once trapped in the dark, spiraling vortex of occultic practices. Everything only goes downward from here!

If a believer in Christ becomes involved in occult activities, God will exercise discipline on His child, *as He does for all sin* (Hebrews 12:5–11). If that child of God becomes so immersed in the occult that they are in danger of casting aside their faith in Christ, God may take the final step of discipline, removing them from that situation and bringing them home to Heaven, through death.

Why be involved with the forces of darkness and the possibility of being oppressed or possessed by murderous, lying evil spirits, *falling under a curse that will then go on to enslave your children and your children's children?* Satan is the *master deceiver*. He and his cohorts know full well the destruction that lies ahead for them and for all who follow in his ways. Don't forget the adage "Misery loves company"!

If you are *not a follower* of Jesus, Satan has no concern regarding your eternal destiny, since *you* make that determination for yourself, *once you reject God's offer of salvation*. And if you believe that you are someone who can dabble or participate in spiritual matters *that do not flow from the throne of God* without falling under the sway and possibly the complete control of Satan, then I am saddened in my spirit to inform you that you are a victim of his *mastery of deception*.

"For our struggle is not against flesh and blood, but against the rulers, against the authorities, against the *powers of this dark world and against the spiritual forces of evil in the heavenly realms*" (Ephesians 6:12, NIV; emphasis added).

Who can stand against such power? Jesus Himself has *already defeated Satan*, but you must turn away from Satan and everything he represents, turning instead to Jesus the Savior if you want to avail yourself of His freedom. Once involved in occultic ideologies there simply remains no other way of escape other than through the person of Jesus and His resurrected power. Instead of being filled with the spirit of darkness, you can be filled with the light of a loving, righteous Holy Spirit!

CHAPTER 8
God's Miraculous Power Living Inside of You

(Set Apart)

Let's start with a brief description of Who God is.

God is strong. He is sure. God is life. He endures!

God is love. He is good. God is just. He is true. God is faithful to the end.

God is light, now breaking in.

He is more than we can grasp. God's eternal, the first and last.

God is the way. He is the truth. He is the grace now crashing through.

He is the Savior, King of kings, Creator of earth and everything.

When His children gather together, God is in that place.

God is the One Who always loved you.

The proof is in His grace!

God is always right on time, and He's returning very soon!
God referred to Himself as *YHWH,* meaning "I AM" (Exodus 3:14).

He created all that is, all that ever was, and all that is to come. Jesus was with God at creation as *the Word,* later manifesting to the world as flesh (a baby born to Mary, a virgin who was impregnated by the power of *Holy Spirit)* (Luke 1:35).

It was through that *Word (Jesus)* that everything was spoken into existence. All things, whether seen or unseen. God spoke (the Word), and the world was framed,

> In the beginning [before all time] was the Word (Christ), and the Word was with God, and the Word was God Himself. He was [continually existing] in the beginning [co-eternally] with God. All things were made and came into existence through Him; and without Him not even one thing was made that has come into being.
>
> John 1:1–3

Holy Spirit, as the third person of *the Holy Trinity* was also present at creation.

> In the beginning God (Elohim[15]) created [by forming from nothing] the heavens and the earth. The earth was formless and void or a waste and emptiness, and darkness was upon the face of the deep [primeval ocean that covered the unformed earth]. The Spirit of God was moving (hovering, brooding) over the face of the waters.
>
> Genesis 1:1–3

The Bible states that we are created in the *image or likeness of God,* our Creator.

> Then God said, "Let Us (Father, Son, Holy Spirit) make man in *Our* image, according to Our likeness *[not physical, but a spiritual personality and moral likeness]*; and let them have complete authority over the fish of the sea, the birds of the air, the cattle, and over the entire earth, and over everything that creeps and crawls on the earth." So God created man in His own image, in the image and likeness of God He created him; male and female He created them.
>
> Genesis 1:26–27 (emphasis added)

---

15. "Elohim" is a Hebrew name for God, and it is plural.

Our being formed in the likeness of *God* also speaks to both *God and* humans as triune beings (three in one). We were created as soul, body, and spirit. The *Holy Trinity is Father, Son and Spirit... Three in One, The Great I Am, or YHWH!* And though we fell from God's presence and fellowship, God has made available, *through the Blood of Jesus,* the way back; hallelujah!

Also, through the blood of Jesus, we have *access* to the same power that resides and operates in Jesus (Who has been glorified and now sits at the right hand of the Father in Heaven).

"Fixing our eyes on Jesus, the pioneer and perfecter of faith. For the joy set before him he endured the cross, scorning its shame, and sat down at the right hand of the throne of God" (Hebrews 12:2, NIV).

The same power that rose Jesus from the dead now lives and operates inside of every believer!

"And if the Spirit of Him who raised Jesus from the dead lives in you, He who raised Christ Jesus from the dead will also give life to your mortal bodies through His Spirit, who lives in you" (Romans 8:11).

So, we were not only created in God's image at creation, but all who surrender their lives to Jesus have the Spirit of Him Who raised Jesus from the dead living in and through them.

Now, I have no earthly idea of what you believe about our existence, but I'm much happier (even elated) to have assurance that I didn't "evolve" from some primordial soup; rather, I was intricately and wonderfully crafted by a loving *Creator, Father God (or Abba, which means "Daddy" in the Hebrew Language).*

My heavenly Father, the Creator, fashioned me in His own image!

"My frame was not hidden from You, When I was being formed in secret, And intricately and skillfully formed [*as if embroidered with many colors*] in the depths of the earth" (Psalm 139:15; emphasis added).

This scripture is in reference to everyone ever born.

It's rather depressing, I think, to imagine that our origins belong to a one-celled organism. I don't know how anyone adhering to this contrived perspective can experience any genuine, intrinsic value or hold any regard for the value of others. How and when did one-celled creatures develop sufficiently to possess thought and intent, let alone good character? Did human character and nobility just spring out of nowhere as we evolved closer to our current human condition? The logic of this escapes me. Grace, justice, mercy and loving-kindness are ethereal and, therefore, must rise from a *source* higher than this mere physical plane. These qualities did not materialize as the result of cellular division and could never have evolved but were ignited by the spark of a *Holy Creator*. Were it not so, the human race would have achieved these characteristics already, after so many "millions of years" of evolution.

Quite to the contrary, there have never been so many wars occurring, all at the same time, throughout the history of the world. Earth is fully immersed in ferocious violence! Where is the fruit of humanity's evolved thinking and behavior? I see only devolution of societies' norms of reasoning and conduct... Indeed, this warping of the human fabric seems to be proceeding downhill like a snowball headed for Hell (growing exponentially)! *O! Evolution, where is your saving grace?*

The *Creator, YHWH,* doesn't leave anything to chance. Everything He has ever done, or ever will do, is fraught with pattern, purpose, and passion. His eye on His soon-coming eternal Kingdom, *YHWH, is* eternal. He has no beginning and no end. He is not constrained by time. (He operates outside of it.) Since He is eternal, we will never reach a point (even in eternity) when we will have discovered *all* there *is* to know about Him. And those who love God, even in eternity, will never be able to discover the depths of His love for His own! We will be engaged in an eternal treasure hunt! Each time we discover a new nugget of God's love, we'll fall on our faces with all the saints and angels, crying, "Holy, holy, holy is the Lord God Almighty." *There is more to God than could ever even be enclosed in words. Words are containers, and YHWH cannot be contained!*

His breath, however, *is* contained within each and every one of us, and I can easily demonstrate that. First, the Bible tells us plainly that, at creation, we received God's very own breath.

"Then the Lord God formed [that is, created the body of] man from the dust of the ground, and *breathed into his nostrils the breath of life*; and the man became a living being [an individual complete in body and spirit]" (Genesis 2:7; emphasis added).

But that's not all. If you will indulge a little creative license here, I believe I can physically prove to you that God's very breath still resides right inside of you! This might sound a little silly at first, but follow along and see if you can hear what I hear as I focus on His Name, *YHWH*.

(Try this by breathing only with your open mouth, *not through your nose*).

First, take a deep breath in, then as you exhale through your mouth, think about the sound "WH." Do you hear that in the whisper of your breath? Now, as you inhale, think about the sound "YH." It's subtle, but did you hear it? Exhale, "WH;" inhale, "YH." Do it a few times in a row.

Exhale and empty yourself of self… Inhale and fill yourself with Creator God!

"In his hand is the soul of every living thing, and *the life breath* of all mortal flesh" (Job 12:10, NAB; emphasis added).

CHAPTER 9
Confident Access to God's Presence and Provision

(The Authority and Power Available to You, as a Believer)

Having been forgiven through our repentance and faith in what Jesus did for us when dying on the cross, we are clothed in God's righteousness (Jesus' Blood), giving us access to the Throne Room of God (the Holy of Holies).

On earth, the Holy of Holies is the most sacred location in the Jewish Synagogue. It is a representation or shadow of the Holy of Holies in Heaven, the most excellent and sacred place, the Throne Room of *YHWH*! Only the High Priest was allowed entry into the Holy of Holies of the Synagogue, and only once a year, in order to sprinkle the sacrificial blood of a slain bull on the altar. This was as atonement for the sins of the whole nation. The Holy of Holies was shielded by a two-layered veil, each layer woven 3.5 inches thick. At the hour of Jesus' death on the cross, the veil to the Holy of Holies was torn in two, from top to bottom, by the hand of God, signifying full access to the Holy of Holies in Heaven through the shed Blood of Jesus Christ! Everyone whose sins have been washed white in the river of Jesus' Blood has been granted the privilege of direct access to the Throne Room of Abba, Father God!

Jesus, Who sits on the right hand of the Father, *advocates on our behalf and prays for us.* He is our High Priest and Advocate! An advocate is someone who speaks on your behalf and in your defense. It is through His shed Blood that we are clothed in righteousness (right standing with God). This, dear fellow believer, is your *confident access to God's presence and provision.*

CHAPTER 10
Equipped for Spiritual Warfare

The Armor of God (Demolishing Satan's Stronghold)

For though we walk in the flesh [as mortal men], we are not carrying on our [spiritual] warfare according to the flesh and using the weapons of man. The weapons of our warfare are not physical [weapons of flesh and blood]. Our weapons are divinely powerful for the destruction of fortresses.

2 Corinthians 10:3–4

God, Who called us, has also equipped us.

For though we live in the world, we do not wage war as the world does. The weapons we fight with are not the weapons of the world. On the contrary, they have *divine power* to demolish strongholds. We demolish arguments and every pretension that sets itself up against the knowledge of God.

2 Corinthians 10:3–5 (NIV; emphasis added)

What are the weapons of every believer's warfare?
1. The truth, power, and authority of God's Word.
2. Holy Spirit's ongoing presence and infilling of your being.
3. A heart that is at peace with God through the Blood of Jesus and full surrender to God's will for your life.
4. Your mind focused on God.

5. Faith in God.
6. Prayer and fasting.
7. Thanksgiving, praise, and worship of God (in this, you enter into the joy of the Lord).

1. The Truth, Power, and Authority of God's Word

When our mouths declare, and our hearts agree, God's Word is a weapon.

"And take the helmet of salvation, and the sword of the Spirit, which is the Word of God" (Ephesians 6:17).

2. Holy Spirit's Ongoing Presence and Infilling

When a believer first repents, making a commitment to live life for Jesus and His kingdom, a deposit of Holy Spirit takes residence inside your body.

> For as many as are the promises of God, in Christ they are [all answered] "Yes." So through Him we say our "Amen" to the glory of God. Now it is God who establishes and confirms us [in joint fellowship] with you in Christ, and who has anointed us [empowering us with the gifts of the Spirit]; it is He who has also put His seal on us [that is, He has appropriated us and certified us as His] and *has given us the [Holy] Spirit in our hearts as a pledge [like a security deposit* to guarantee the fulfillment of His promise of eternal life].
>
> 2 Corinthians 1:20–22 (emphasis added)

In Ephesians 5:18, we're commanded not to be drunk with wine, but let's *not* just focus on the beginning of this verse and leave off the rest.

"And don't get drunk with wine, which leads to reckless actions, *but be filled by the Spirit*" (Ephesians 5:18, HCSB; emphasis added).

Not only are you commanded not to be drunk, but you're *also commanded* to be filled with Holy Spirit. The original Greek text for the word "filled" in this verse means to be *continually filled.*

So, you are to be continually refilled with Holy Spirit each new day. The purposes of the fullness of Holy Spirit are wonderful and varied, some of which are the following: counselor, comforter, teacher, intercessor, your source of holy boldness, stamina, and supernatural strength for waging supernatural war. Holy Spirit will cause you to pause and think when your flesh tells you to react out of anger or fear. Holy Spirit also draws you to Jesus and brings to your memory just the right scripture that you have memorized at just the right moment for victory over temptation or trial. If you belong to Jesus, Holy Spirit is living inside of you. He communicates with your most inner being, sometimes perceived as a still, small voice or a strong impression or feeling of heaviness when you are tempted to sin or threatened by the enemy. Can you see why it's essential to be filled afresh every day? In the presence of God is a fresh anointing of God's Holy Spirit!

There's no other way to be filled afresh other than spending time alone with God!

(For detailed information on the infilling of Holy Spirit, read the first three chapters of the book of Acts).

3. Your Heart at Peace with God, through the Blood of Jesus and *Surrendering* to God's Will for Your Life (Confidence in His Holy Presence)

When your heart is clean, you have the confidence to count on God's promises in His Word, claiming each promise as your own. You *cannot* walk in this confidence when you continue practicing the sins that separate you from His presence. Ask God to forgive you and strengthen you with His love to help you *do His will.*

4. Your Mind Focused on God

Satan's battlefield is in your mind!

"Among them the god of this world [Satan] has blinded the minds of the unbelieving to prevent them from seeing the illuminating light of the gospel of the glory of Christ, who is the image of God" (2 Corinthians 4:4).

And for those belonging to Christ, we are warned.

"So *prepare your minds for action, be completely sober* [in spirit—steadfast, self-disciplined, spiritually and morally alert], fix your hope completely on the grace [of God] that is coming to you when Jesus Christ is revealed" (1 Peter 1:14; emphasis added).

5. Faith in God

Simply put, faith is counting God as faithful in all of His promises and everything He declares!

"If we are faithless, He remains faithful [true to His word and His righteous character], for He cannot deny Himself" (2 Timothy 2:13).

6. Prayer and Fasting

Prayer and fasting are not optional in the effective Christian life. Jesus, when discussing prayer and fasting with His disciples, obviously expected them to do both, or He would have made the following statement as a suggestion rather than phrasing it as *something expected.*

> Also, *when* you pray, do not be like the hypocrites; for they love to pray [publicly] standing in the synagogues and on the corners of the streets so that they may be seen by men. I assure you and most solemnly say to you, they [already] have their reward in full. But *when* you pray, go into your most private room, close the door and pray to your Father who is in secret, and your Father who sees [what is done] in secret will reward you.
>
> Matthew 6:5–6 (emphasis added)

And *whenever* you are fasting, do not look gloomy like the hypocrites, for they put on a sad and dismal face [like actors, discoloring their faces with ashes or dirt] so that their fasting may be seen by men. I assure you and most solemnly say to you, they [already] have their reward in full. But *when* you fast, put oil on your head [as you normally would to groom your hair] and wash your face so that your fasting will not be noticed by people, but by your Father who is in secret; and your Father who sees [what is done] in secret will reward you.

Matthew 6:16–18 (emphasis added)

Please notice in the scriptures above that the emphasized words are "when" and "whenever," not "if." Each phrase stated by Jesus here demonstrates that He clearly expected His followers to pray and fast.

7. Praise and Worship of God Is a Weapon

About midnight Paul and Silas were praying and singing hymns to God, and the other prisoners were listening to them. Suddenly there was such a violent earthquake that the foundations of the prison were shaken. At once all the prison doors flew open, and everyone's chains came loose.

Acts 16:25–26 (NIV)

Praise as a weapon is very effective in shoving back the forces of evil. It is also very effective in helping you to better focus on God in your quiet time with Him and in your daily life. Praise helps you to focus on God and thus have better intimate communication with Him and to hear God's voice. Hearing God's voice is the most important part of your fellowship time with Him!

"The sheep that are My own hear My voice and listen to Me; I know them, and they follow Me" (John 10:27).

Praise and worship of God also help you to know Him in dynamic and personal ways rather than just knowing about God.

The Armor of God

Ephesians 6 challenges us to put on the *full* armor of God.
- The belt of truth
- The breastplate of righteousness
- The readiness that comes through the preparation of the gospel of peace (regular study of God's Word)
- The shield of faith
- The helmet of salvation
- The sword that the spirit wields (the Word of God)
- The practice of prayer

Each piece of armor is essential to your victory over Satan. Going without even one piece is as ineffective as having no armor at all. It's a package deal. Trying to stand against the spiritual forces of darkness without each piece would compare to driving a car with no power source or no steering mechanism… that's not going to work. That is why the Bible instructs us regarding the Belt of Truth. What we do for God must be done in truth.

The Belt of Truth

During biblical days, men wore garments that were long and loose, such as a tunic. This clothing could be cumbersome during any physical work, so it was gathered and tucked into the belt during physical exertion. This is a perfect analogy that points to the necessity of operating within the boundaries of truth if you are to accomplish God's will on this earth. The Bible says that Jesus *is* truth, making it evident that you must first be *in* Christ Jesus to work for God's kingdom and wield His power. That is why the Bible instructs you regarding the Belt of Truth. What you do for God must be done in truth. You must walk in truth and be genuine with God, yourself, and others if you are to operate in God's power and accomplish the work that He has set before you for this day.

What protection is offered through the Belt of Truth?

- Protection from error: Error happens when the truth of God's Word is compromised by misinterpretation, misrepresentation, or misunderstanding. The resulting error may seem accurate because it is so close to the truth. The error causes you to question what God has said and may lead you astray.
- Protection from deception: Deception is an out-and-out lie someone else tries to convince you to believe. Some lies are so clever that you may be tricked into thinking it is true.
- Protection from deceit: Deceit is when you try to get someone else to accept a lie that you choose to tell.
- Protection from illusion or delusion: An illusion is seeing something other than what is actually there. An example would be a person or spirit being who wants to harm you or hurt you, acting as though they are kind or beneficial in order to win your trust. A delusion would be a truth that you refuse to see about yourself and the lies you tell yourself to avoid dealing with what you don't want to face. Some people refer to this as denial.

The Breastplate of Righteousness

Where does your body experience the sensation of sheer joy or the stabbing pain of a broken heart? It is in your chest area. Of course, your heart muscle isn't actually injured, but the emotional pain or ecstasy you experience flows from that core place of your being. And your lungs? Again, located in the same area. When the heavenly Father created Adam, He breathed into him His very own breath, and Adam came to life (Genesis 2:7). Think about it; every extreme of joy and pain and the very breath of God reside in the vulnerable area of your breast. God has provided His children with the most excellent shield for our protection. Ephesians 6:14 tells believers to clad themselves in the breastplate of righteousness. Notice, God doesn't do it for you but tells *you* to put it on. You are clothing yourself or putting on the righteousness of Jesus. He becomes your righteousness when you are born again (your spirit is made new).

You aren't righteous by *trying to be good*, no; it takes place because, *through your faith in Jesus*, you are covered in His Blood; then, through a daily vivid connection with Jesus via a loving and consistent relationship, you are constantly renewed and refined unto holiness. It is a process, but God calls each and every one of His children to holiness. When I consider the purity and holiness of *YHWH*, the possibility of my being holy leaves me feeling hopeless of ever achieving this on my own. Do you feel that way? I'm inclined to believe that Father God is pleased with this conclusion. In fact, without the regenerative power found within the wisdom of the Bible and the dynamic working of Holy Spirit in your life, no one can ever even come close to holiness. It is a miracle of God's sovereignty and love.

"All of us like sheep have gone astray, We have turned, each one, to his own way; But the Lord has caused the wickedness of us all [our sin, our injustice, our wrongdoing] To fall on Him [instead of us]" (Isaiah 53:6).

"But like the Holy One who called you, be holy yourselves in all your conduct [be set apart from the world by your godly character and moral courage]; because it is written, 'You shall be holy (set apart), for I am holy'" (1 Peter 1:15–16).

Being clothed in His righteousness, you are in right standing with God.

This is your confident access to the Throne of God!

It is the righteousness and love of Jesus that I want people to see whenever I interact with them. I pray that you do—or will soon want to—*truly* know Him, experiencing in your own life His all-encompassing, healing love. Pursuing and walking in God's righteousness brings you into a position of favor with God. It is the very thing that Satan most hates and will work at tearing down. He wants everyone to believe that our relationship with God is dependent upon *what we do* for Him rather than what He has already done for us through His Son, Jesus.

Another trick of Satan is to bring up past sins, trying to inflict shame on you for what has already been forgiven. Knowing that shame interferes with being close to Jesus, Satan would have me forget that I am clothed in the righteousness of Jesus, and it is *His* righteousness that God sees when He looks at me. Micah 7:19 says that *God cast our sin into the depths of the sea!*

It's like launching a rocket at the enemy when, in the power of Holy Spirit, you declare this verse in Micah 7:19 to Satan! He will turn and run. Declare this scripture *out loud* to Satan whenever he parades your past in front of you. This is referred to as making a proclamation, sometimes called a declaration. It is an integral ingredient in your effective prayer life! Many scriptures are useful weapons against Satan's temptation and attacks, but you must *first memorize* them. Don't wait to start memorizing scriptures. Satan will push hard to dissuade you from this discipline because it is so incredibly powerful. He knows that scripture that is committed to memory will guard your heart, mind, and body.

Proclaim each day that you are clothed in the breastplate of righteousness. Proclaiming *out loud* where you stand with God is a powerful reminder to yourself and Satan. I announce out loud *every piece of armor* as I focus on God cladding me in His strength, protection, and goodness. I do not doubt that Satan knows that I understand where I stand with my Lord. I do not doubt that the enemy sees God's covering over me because I have reminded him in detail! The righteousness of Jesus, in which I am clothed, is my supreme protection from the accuser of my soul. I am *confident in drawing near to Father God* because I know I am accepted into His presence. Today, I won't let the enemy of my soul shame me out of that closeness to Jesus, sweeter than anything I've ever known!

Feet Shod with the Preparation of the Gospel of Peace

What is the preparation of the gospel of peace?

Just about every busy restaurant has a prep cook. They'll gather all the necessary ingredients, chop, weigh, mix, sort, and store everything for later use. All the ingredients and the way they merge, bringing each dish together, are committed to memory so that the head chef has the means to achieve the desired results: *a masterpiece. You are the prep cook; Holy Spirit is the Master Chef!*

God has instructed us to study to show ourselves approved to rightly handle the Word of God. This means you must regularly read, study, and memorize scriptures, asking Holy Spirit to guide you into truth and revelation knowledge each time you open it. Holy Spirit is a faithful teacher that will never ever lead you into error because God *wants* you to know His truth and hide it in your heart.

"Be diligent to present yourself approved to God, a worker who does not need to be ashamed, *rightly dividing the word of truth*" (2 Timothy 2:15, NKJV; emphasis added).

Remember this: Satan will always try to interfere with your reading or understanding of the Word of God. I don't mean listening to some other person's teaching. I'm talking about personal study time, alone with God. Satan knows this is how God directly delivers a perfectly tailored Word of instruction or encouragement (meant just for you). Satan and all of his cohorts quake at the sight or sound of God's Word! You have the right and the power *in the Name of Jesus* to cancel their assignment of interference, and you *should, by all means, use it!*

Reading both the New and Old Testament will give the firmest grasp on what the gospel of Christ is and the full meaning of its eternal benefits and responsibilities. You must first experience the peace and liberty found by embracing and receiving the gospel as your own before you have anything of God's Kingdom to share with others. How can you share His peace if you are wrought up with anxiety? Relief for anxiety is found in the Living Words of the Bible. God can and does, through the water of His Word, wash your mind clean of fear and fill you with His inexplicable peace in the midst of *any* and every circumstance. But that peace comes only through personal knowledge of what God has proclaimed to you and applying that knowledge to the way you live and view life.

This liberates you to relish in the joy of the Lord!

The gospel is designed with infinite wisdom, purchased at an enormous price, the Blood of Jesus, and conveyed by the infinite power of Holy Spirit. *YHWH* never intended His people to be robots going through the motions of life. Jesus came that you might have life, have it abundantly, and in *His power* be motivated... The believers who march encounter rugged terrain. We charge into spiritual conflict. We are stormed with weapons and require impenetrable footwear, footwear that comes from a loving and wise King. The believer's feet are shod with a *divine preparation*. Every portion of the gospel is from *God*, and all the impact that makes it a gospel of peace is *found in a personal, intimate relationship with Him.* I cannot think of a more protective material for the shoes of the soldier than the gospel of peace and the peace that grows *out of* the gospel.

The blessings of the gospel can't be calculated. Yet, it is *free*! It is an everlasting and pure gospel! From God's peace, your shoes are prepared with *that which you trample the lion and the cobra* (Psalms 91:13, Luke 10:19). This shoe means that you know that as the Lord holds you in His sight, His gaze is full of infinite, undivided compassion and affection. He sees you *through Jesus* as cleansed from every speck of sin. *"Accepted in the Beloved"* (Ephesians 1:3–6). Not only accepted, but the Lord *waits for and delights in your time spent with Him.* When you know that you can come shamelessly before the Lord because you have peace with Him, your *confidence* is bolstered, fortifying your victory over all of the spiritual forces of darkness.

The Shield of Faith

"The shield of faith is constructed in such a way as to fend off any fiery missile your enemy sends your way" (Derek Prince).

Before we look at *the shield of faith* in detail, it seems that the currently popularized use of the word *"faith"* and its meaning bears some discussion. There are similar definitions for faith throughout various dictionaries, but taken together they simply mean *complete confidence in someone or something*.

Lately, we see numerous inspirational postings on social media, or wall decor encouraging a reader to have faith, but exactly what are we having faith in? Is it faith when you enter an elevator, push the number five button, and expect to arrive at the fifth floor? Do you trust the integrity of the manufacturer, installers, and the last inspector's evaluation of its safety? Is that really faith? I think not. Faith proceeds from your heart. Hope is a product of your mind. You consider the odds of the elevator working as intended and *hope* that all of the above-mentioned people connected to its function were properly carrying out their duties. But you don't regard them in your heart as trustworthy and competent because you don't even *know them* or the companies employing them. You've seen this elevator operate in the past with no issues, so you step on and take the ride, *hoping* it correctly functions.

Now, if the elevator manufacturing plant was owned by your father, and you were present during installation and later inspections, you would then have *substantial* reason to have faith in that particular equipment. Do you see the difference between faith and hope? *It is within an intimate relationship that faith is developed.*

Listen to what the Bible says about faith in Hebrews 11:1 (NKJV, emphasis added): "Now faith is the *substance* of things hoped for, the evidence of things not seen."

Obviously, the shield of faith is a spiritual type of faith based on an invisible *Creator* Who tells us in His Word that He saves, protects, and cares for the ones who belong to Him. You do not see Him, yet you have faith in Him.

"Jesus said to him, 'Because you have seen Me, do you now believe? Blessed [happy, spiritually secure, and favored by God] are they who did not see [Me] and yet believed [in Me]'" (John 20:29).

If you can see something, you do not need faith.

The Creator gave you senses to navigate the seen, physical realm. He gives faith to *navigate the unseen, spiritual realm* to those who seek Him.

Faith brings spiritual sight.

The Bible says the following about faith:

"But without faith it is impossible to [walk with God and] please Him, for whoever comes [near] to God must [necessarily] believe that God exists and that He rewards those who [earnestly and diligently] seek Him" (Hebrews 11:6).

So, how do you obtain faith in the Creator God?

If you are asking how to have faith in God, then you already have *a measure* of faith. You can't desire something from someone unless you believe that this "someone" exists. Listen to what Jesus said about *a measure of faith*.

> And the Lord said, "If you have [confident, abiding] faith in God [even as small] as a mustard seed, you could say to this mulberry tree [which has very strong roots], 'Be pulled up by the roots and be planted in the sea'; and [if the request was in agreement with the will of God] it would have obeyed you."
>
> Luke 17:6

The mustard seed is tiny (less than an inch in diameter), yet the full-grown tree can reach up to thirty feet tall, with a twenty-foot-wide canopy. So, even if your faith starts out tiny, it won't remain that way for long because God is in charge of growing your faith. He will *faithfully* bring you to and through situations that grow your faith (sometimes exponentially). Some places in the Bible talk about *great faith*.

Let's return to the elevator analogy for a moment. Remember the part about the elevator manufacturer being your father? Because you know your father well, you know that he is honest and kind, you trust him and rely on him, and you have great faith in him and confidence in his reliability. But suppose you were only acquainted with the manufacturer through what you had read or heard about him. Your level of trust in his product would not hold nearly the strength of your confidence in your father. You see, it is in personally knowing and spending time in a relationship with God that we come to have *great faith*. Throughout every test and trial, when God has stood by you or rescued you from grave danger, *the substance* of your faith grows bigger and stronger.

"Now faith is the *substance* of things hoped for, the evidence of things not seen" (Hebrews 11:1, NKJV; emphasis added).

In the following verse, Jesus had cursed a fig tree, and it withered and died immediately. The reason He cursed it isn't the point here. The point is that what He spoke to the fig tree had a definite result that surprised His disciples, who at this point in Jesus' ministry had only tiny faith.

> Jesus replied to them, "I assure you and most solemnly say to you, if you have faith [personal trust and confidence in Me] and do not doubt or allow yourself to be drawn in two directions, you will not only do what was done to the fig tree, but even if you say to this mountain, 'Be taken up and thrown into the sea,' it will happen [if God wills it]. And whatever you ask for in prayer, believing, you will receive."
>
> Matthew 21:21–22

In summary, you must have faith that God exists to come to Him and learn His will and way for your life. We also discussed that even if you start off a relationship with God having only the tiniest seed of faith, He will grow you in your faith, even to the point of having great faith (which He wants all His children to have)! With that discussion of faith under our belts, let's focus on the *shield of faith* that extinguishes all the fiery missiles of the enemy.

In Ephesians 6, when Paul discussed being clad in God's armor, he referred to the Roman Foot Soldier's battle armor. The shield Paul described was the size of a door, providing coverage over the front side of the entire body. Each soldier's shield could be joined side by side, all along the front rank, to form an almost impenetrable wall of defense or offense against the opposing army.

"And with these, take to you the shield of faith, that with it you may have the power to quench all of the blazing bolts of The Evil One" (Ephesians 6:16, ABPE).

The Helmet of Salvation

The next vital piece of armor is *the helmet of salvation,* with which the soldier of God protects their mind. The believer's mind is the main battlefield of Satan. But your helmet *identifies you* to the enemy as *belonging to Jesus.* (Jesus is our head.) You protect your thoughts and ideas by weighing them against what God has spoken in His written Word. If the "little voices in your head" don't line up with what scripture has already proclaimed, you can be certain those thoughts are from the enemy. You have the right and authority to bind Satan in the name of Jesus and tell him to leave, *and you should!*

Additionally, you must guard what enters your mind through your eye and ear gate. Don't be fooled into believing you can indulge in media and entertainment that would embarrass you if the Lord were in the room. *He is in the room* if you belong to Him because He lives inside of you. Wherever you go, He goes with you. Let this truth be at the front of your mind to protect you from the corruption of worldly or demonic forms of entertainment. Also, examine your personal relationships, asking God to separate you from those who will drag you down and away from your relationship with your Savior and King, Jesus.

"Do not be deceived: 'Bad company corrupts good morals'" (1 Corinthians 15:33).

"So prepare your minds for action, be completely sober [in spirit—steadfast, self-disciplined, spiritually and morally alert], fix your hope completely on the grace [of God] that is coming to you when Jesus Christ is revealed" (1 Peter 1:13).

The Sword That the Spirit Wields (The Word of God)

> For the word of God is living and active and full of power [making it operative, energizing, and effective]. It is sharper than any two-edged sword, penetrating as far as the division of the soul and spirit [the completeness of a person], and of both joints and marrow [the deepest parts of our nature], exposing and judging the very thoughts and intentions of the heart.
>
> Hebrews 4:12

The Word of God is *YHWH's* love letter to the world. The Bible holds instructions regarding living your life in the power and purpose of God's will. It tells Who God is and how to know Him intimately. The Word of God is *God-breathed,* spoken through Holy Spirit to the spirit and soul of each writer of its contents. Jesus, in the Bible, is referred to as the Word because His Word did not spring from any man. The Word of God holds the power of life and death and everything in between. To those who love it, when the Bible is read and applied to our lives, it contains the transformative power to bring life to dry bones.

> Again He said to me, "Prophesy to these bones, and say to them, 'O dry bones, hear the word of the Lord! Thus says the Lord God to these bones: "Surely I will cause breath to enter into you, and you shall live. I will put sinews on you and bring flesh upon you, cover you with skin and put breath in you; and you shall live. Then you shall know that I am the Lord.""

> So I prophesied as I was commanded; and as I prophesied, there was a noise, and suddenly a rattling; and the bones came together, bone to bone. Indeed, as I looked, the sinews and the flesh came upon them, and the skin covered them over; but there was no breath in them.
>
> Also He said to me, "Prophesy to the breath, prophesy, son of man, and say to the breath, 'Thus says the Lord God: "Come from the four winds, O breath, and breathe on these slain, that they may live."'" So I prophesied as He commanded me, and breath came into them, and they lived, and stood upon their feet, an exceedingly great army.
>
> Ezekiel 37:4–10 (NKJV)

God's Word has the power to bring beauty to ashes in lives that have been transformed by His gospel.

"To console those who mourn in Zion, To give them beauty for ashes, The oil of joy for mourning, The garment of praise for the spirit of heaviness; That they may be called trees of righteousness, The planting of the Lord, that He may be glorified" (Isaiah 61:3, NKJV).

The spoken Word of the Lord even has the power to raise the dead and drive out demons!

> Then Jesus, again groaning in Himself, came to the tomb. It was a cave, and a stone lay against it. Jesus said, "Take away the stone."
>
> Martha, the sister of him who was dead, said to Him, "Lord, by this time there is a stench, for he has been dead four days."
>
> Jesus said to her, "Did I not say to you that if you would believe you would see the glory of God?" Then they took away the stone from the place where the dead man was lying. And Jesus lifted up His eyes and said, "Father, I thank You that You have heard Me. And I know that You always hear Me, but because of the people who are standing by I said this, that they may believe that You sent Me." Now when He had said these things, He cried with a loud voice, "Lazarus, come

forth!" And he who had died came out bound hand and foot with graveclothes, and his face was wrapped with a cloth. Jesus said to them, "Loose him, and let him go."

John 11:38–44 (NKJV)

Although we have now listed and briefly explained how we are to be covered in God's armor, let us *not* forget the discussion of prayer, which Paul includes in our process of waging war against the devil. We need to be clothed in God's armor, but we also need to be *covered in prayer*!

CHAPTER 11
The Practice of Prayer and Fasting

"Rejoicing in hope, patient in tribulation, continuing steadfastly in prayer" (Romans 12:12, NKJV).

"With all prayer and petition pray [with specific requests] at all times [on every occasion and in every season] in the Spirit, and with this in view, stay alert with all perseverance and petition [interceding in prayer] for all God's people" (Ephesians 6:18).

The Power of Prayer

First, let's discuss what prayer *isn't*.

- Prayer is not how you get God to do what you want. (You need first to know what God wants for you and pray according to His perfect desires, convinced of His goodness and kindness toward you.)
- Prayer is not reciting strings of religious words, ideals, or requests,
- Prayer is not petitioning God through another person, such as a priest. Or saint.

Jesus is the High Priest of every believer.

Now the main point of what we have to say is this: *we have such a High Priest*, [the Christ] who is seated [in the place of honor] at the right hand of the throne of the Majesty (God) in heaven, *a Minister (Officiating Priest)* in the holy places and *in the true tabernacle*, which is erected not by man, but by the Lord.

Hebrews 8:1–2 (emphasis added)

Believers who come humbly to God are covered in the Blood of Jesus and, because of this, have direct access to the Throne Room of God!

What *is* prayer?

Prayer is how the Lord moves through us to supernaturally impact the spiritual and physical realm, according to God's will and under the direction of Holy Spirit.

I realize that this definition sounds quite lofty, but it is actually quite simple if you just realize that effective prayer is hinged on praying according to what God wills rather than according to your own will. Once this becomes the genuine attitude of your heart, when offered in faith, such prayers produce dynamic and often miraculous results! Prayer is laying your heart bare to our Father God, *Abba* (Hebrew for "daddy").

Consider the prayer of Jesus just before His arrest and His appointed suffering. Jesus, Who walked the earth fully human, poured out His heart to His Father, completely wrought up in mental torment because He knew what lay ahead for Him in the next few hours of His life. He faced not only demonically cruel physical torture but *also* the full weight of mental anguish and shame of every person to have ever walked the face of this planet. Bearing even the sin and vile insanity of wicked dictators such as Kim Jong Il, Saddam Hussein, Idi Amin, and Hitler, as well as other brutal people, such as serial killers, down through the ages.

Father God laid all the filth and shame of the sin of all who ever lived (including you and me) squarely on the shoulders of His only Son, and then He turned away! *God cannot look at sin.*

All of Heaven Wept

> And He came out and went, as was His habit, to the Mount of Olives; and the disciples followed Him. When He arrived at the place [called Gethsemane], He said to them, "Pray continually that you may not fall into temptation." And He withdrew from them about a stone's throw, and knelt down

and prayed, saying, "Father, if You are willing, remove this cup [of divine wrath] from Me; yet not My will, but [always] Yours be done." Now an angel appeared to Him from heaven, strengthening Him. *And being in agony [deeply distressed and anguished; almost to the point of death], He prayed more intently; and His sweat became like drops of blood, falling down on the ground.* When He rose from prayer, He came to the disciples and found them sleeping from sorrow, and He said to them, "Why are you sleeping? Get up and pray that you may not fall into temptation."

Luke 22:39–46 (emphasis added)

When God poured out His wrath on His only Son, placing the sin of everyone on Him, Jesus' sweet fellowship with His Father was completely severed… This was the most unbearable thing that He suffered. For all eternity past, Jesus had been one with the Father and Spirit until He left His throne in glory to take on the form of a man. And the moment all that sin alighted on Jesus was the darkest time in all of history!

> From the sixth hour until the ninth hour darkness came over all the land. At the ninth hour, Jesus cried out in a loud voice, "Eloi, Eloi, lema sabachthani?" which means, *"My God, My God, why have You forsaken Me?"*
>
> When some of those standing nearby heard this, they said, "Behold, He is calling Elijah."
>
> And someone ran and filled a sponge with sour wine. He put it on a reed and held it up for Jesus to drink, saying, "Leave Him alone. Let us see if Elijah comes to take Him down."
>
> But Jesus let out a loud cry and breathed His last. *And the veil of the temple was torn in two from top to bottom.*
>
> Mark 15:33–37 (BSB; emphasis added)

Back up and read Mark 22 again. Look at the words of Jesus as He pours out His heart to His *heavenly Father*. He asks for what He yearns: relief from the cup He must drink if He is to conquer death and save the world. In sheer dread, He sweats drops of Blood, yet humbly, He places His Father's will above His own. An angel comes, bringing Him comfort and strength.

Jesus is our flawless example of perfect submission in prayer. Place your requests before God, asking Him to show you His will in any matter, humbly obeying His lead, and leaving the outcome completely in His hands.

If prayer seems daunting and you wouldn't mind some pointers, here you go:

Start with reading your Bible, or listening to and singing some praise music, putting you in a more spiritual frame of mind. Keep your prayer simple and in the style of an actual conversation with someone you dearly love. Prayer is having a discussion with God, remembering to approach His holy presence through thanksgiving, praise and worship.

CHAPTER 12
The Practice of Thanksgiving, Praise, and Worship

Thanksgiving takes your mind off of problems, creating focused attention on all the good things God has done and taking focus off of your circumstances.

Praise helps bring your focus onto God's wonderful attributes, such as His beauty, majesty, power, grace, and love. Praise raises your consciousness to a higher level, helping you to access the very presence of God and His Throne Room, where you enter into worship. Worship isn't something you proclaim or say (that's praise). Worship is an attitude of humility that is experienced in God's presence. It is a posture of adoration with your face bowed, or on your knees, with your body bowed to the floor, or stretched out, face to the floor. Here, in worship, is where you find power for answered prayer, wisdom for the day or the hour, spiritual insight, and revelation; it is the place where you are able to hear God's voice in your heart and feel His love wrapped all around you!

- Prayer is listening in stillness and basking in His presence, hearing His voice, and responding to God's direction.
- Prayer is interceding for others and presenting your personal needs to Him.
- Prayer is declaring or proclaiming what is contained in His Word over every person, circumstance, and enemy.

Here's a great example of declaring God's Word over a person. Let's look at the scripture as it's written in the Bible, and then I will rewrite it, using a person's name in the place of pronouns. Since I love declaring God's Word over my own life, I'll substitute my name for the pronouns written in the Bible; you should do the same with the name of whomever you're praying for.

Here's the original scripture:

> I pray that out of his glorious riches he may strengthen you with power through his Spirit in your inner being, so that Christ may dwell in your hearts through faith. And I pray that you, being rooted and established in love, may have power, together with all the Lord's holy people, to grasp how wide and long and high and deep is the love of Christ, and to know this love that surpasses knowledge—that you may be filled to the measure of all the fullness of God.
>
> Ephesians 3:16–18 (NIV)

Now, here is that scripture prayed with my name inserted: This is how you would pray this scripture for someone else (intercession). When praying directly for yourself, you use the pronouns "me" and "I" rather than a name.

Try it… it may move you to tears if you've never prayed actual Scripture verses out loud.

I pray that out of His glorious riches, He may strengthen Connie with power through His Spirit in her inner being so that Christ may dwell in Connie's heart through faith. And I pray that Connie, being rooted and established in love, may have power, together with all the Lord's holy people, to grasp how wide and long and high and deep is the love of Christ and to know this love that surpasses knowledge—that Connie may be filled to the measure of all the fullness of God.

There are few things in the universe matching the power of praying God's Word over yours, or anyone's life, or any circumstance. You can be absolutely certain that you are praying *in God's will* when praying Scripture over a person or situation. *YHWH* promises in His Word that if you pray in faith, according to His will, you will *have* what you ask for. This is marvelous news (John 14:13)!

I think it could be helpful to add a little about my personal experience in growing an effective and powerful prayer life.

Now, *had I known* about *this* when I first set out to learn how to pray, it would have been quite helpful, so I will start with the most important information about learning how to pray, which is to request the assistance of Holy Spirit in your efforts. You can simply say, "Holy Spirit, teach me to pray," and He will…O! Yes, He will. Hallelujah! You won't find a better teacher in all the universe.

Not realizing that I could enlist the help of Holy Spirit, this was my approach: I read prayers published by others and then prayed them out loud. Probably one of the best publications I found was a tiny little book called *The Prayer of Jabez*. In this book, I found out that there are verses all throughout the Bible that are prayers or that their words can be paraphrased into prayers. Let me tell you when I started praying these scriptures out loud, over and over again, day after day, not only had I memorized a lot of Bible verses, but I started experiencing dynamic and remarkable answers to prayers. This was no coincidence because, for the first time ever, I was witnessing the power of God in my life, in resisting temptation and clearing my mind of the rubble of fear and doubt.

Gradually learning how to pray effectively became the first real turning point in my walk with God. It was regular study of God's Word, finding the beautiful nuggets of truth that always bring liberty and putting those truths to work in my prayers that broke the cycle of defeat. The Word of God contains *supernatural, transformative power. I attest to that!* I finally experienced freedom from constantly sliding back into the choices and behaviors that always beat me down, resulting in defeat. My first taste of experiencing God's power in my life was so satisfying and just what I had been yearning for. It is what made the real difference, thus causing God's power to erupt in my life. It is faithfully (habitually) looking into God's Word, searching for His truth like my life depended on it, and starting the practice of regular prayer. These two disciplines are what is meant by time spent alone with God. The life-energizing, powerful results are what I had been looking for all along: a vibrant and exciting relationship with Abba Father, the overwhelming love of Jesus, and the constant presence and guidance of Holy Spirit!

By no means am I some kind of expert in prayer, so let me point you in the direction of some ministers and teachers of God who taught me so much, and I think they will do the same for you. For additional guidance in building an effective prayer life, I want to recommend the late Dr. Charles Stanley's book *When You Don't Know What to Pray*. Dr. Stanley's Ministry (*In Touch Ministries*) can also be found on YouTube, where you will find teachings on practical biblical lessons that apply to everyday life. A few other excellent Bible teachers whose videos can be found on YouTube and whose teachings are in books are the late brother Derek Prince (*Derek Prince Ministries*), John Bevere (*Messenger International Ministries*), Dr. David Jeremiah (*Turning Point Ministries*), and Amir Tsarfati (*Behold Israel*).

There are certainly some other solid ministries, but I think this list can certainly get you off to a good start! You will also find some of these ministries on television or the internet, but please ask God to guide you *into all truth* when searching for ministries other than those listed here. Satan does not want you to walk in God's truth, and there are a lot of false teachers these days, *just as the Bible predicted would happen in the last days.*

> For the time will come when people will not tolerate sound doctrine and accurate instruction [that challenges them with God's truth]; but wanting to have their ears tickled [with something pleasing], they will accumulate for themselves [many] teachers [one after another, chosen] to satisfy their own desires and to support the errors they hold.
>
> 2 Timothy 4:3

I pray that Holy Spirit keeps you from error, guiding you into all truth!

Since the next section of this book deals with the practice of fasting, I can also recommend a terrific book that will totally familiarize you with what it means to fast unto the Lord and the dynamic power and benefits that grow out of this practice. The book is called *Fasting (opening the door to a deeper, more intimate, more powerful relationship with God)* by Jentezen Franklin.

Derek Prince also published a booklet on fasting to the Lord called *How to Fast Successfully*.

The Practice of Fasting

Fasting unto God is quite different than fasting to cleanse your body. Effective fasting will cleanse your body, yes, but that is not your motive in a *holy fast*. Fasting unto God is how you humble yourself before Him and, at the same time, discipline your flesh unto God's will.

Doing a word search in the Bible, you'll find "fast" or "fasting" multiple times throughout the entire text. It was a regular Judeo-Christian discipline that sadly fell out of practice. Seeking forgiveness or the release of God's supernatural power into the physical realm, or seeking God's direction or wisdom were the usual reasons mentioned for fasting in the Bible; however, there are also times when God called the nation to fast (corporate fasting). When fasting unto God, the time you normally spend preparing food and eating is spent in prayer and meditation on God's Word. If you have a health condition preventing you from skipping meals, there are partial fasts, such as the Daniel Fast (explanations are available online, but it is really just eating only vegetables and fruit and drinking only water). As an alternative, you can abstain from social media and television for a specific period of time. You will be amazed at the number of hours this discipline frees up for prayer and Bible study!

Fasting really gets down to an attitude of your heart.

The attitude God looks for is…humility.

Until 2010, I had never heard of any teaching on *holy fasting*. Pastor David Chapman first taught me about fasting as a corporate endeavor (members of our church fasted for twenty-one days at the same time). I'm so grateful for his teaching! It caused my heart to leap because, listening to his teachings on fasting, I knew that this was how to go even deeper into my faith and intimacy with my Creator and Savior. For this, I was desperate! Would you like to know what will happen to you if you get desperate for more of God? God showed up in my life during my first fast in ways that I had never dreamed possible. I was given the strength of my spirit, the impact, and the miraculous power of Heaven on earth. God's Holy Spirit living inside of me grew from a portion to a fullness that spilled over into every aspect of who I am! As of this writing, I'm worshiping and fasting with the congregation of LifePoint Church in DeLand, Florida. We have the privilege of having a pastor who leads us in corporate fasting every January and September. We fast for twenty-one days and meet before daybreak each morning of the fast for corporate prayer.

Pastor Don Jagers, we as a church body are so grateful for your faithfulness to God's truth and Kingdom principles; thank you! I pray that every follower of Jesus is led to a congregation that realizes and pursues the power and blessing of God through prayer and fasting!

CHAPTER 13
My Testimony

I can't think of a better way than with my testimony of what God did and continues doing in my life since my return from the "Land of the Prodigal" (not a physical place), a spiritual void into which any child of God can plunge by turning from God to the things of this world and living a life of carless foolishness.

Jesus told a poignant story about a prodigal child in Luke 15:11–24 (NIV; emphasis added):

> The Parable of the Lost Son
>
> Jesus continued: "There was a man who had two sons. The younger one said to his father, 'Father, give me my share of the estate.' So he divided his property between them.
>
> "Not long after that, the younger son got together all he had, set off for a distant country and there squandered his wealth in wild living. After he had spent everything, there was a severe famine in that whole country, and he began to be in need. So he went and hired himself out to a citizen of that country, who sent him to his fields to feed pigs. He longed to fill his stomach with the pods that the pigs were eating, but no one gave him anything.
>
> "When he came to his senses, he said, 'How many of my father's hired servants have food to spare, and here I am starving to death! I will set out and go back to my father and say to him: Father, I have sinned against heaven and against you. I am no longer worthy to be called your son; make me like one of your hired servants.' So he got up and went to his father.

"But while he was still a long way off, *his father saw him and was filled with compassion for him; he ran to his son, threw his arms around him and kissed him.*

"The son said to him, 'Father, I have sinned against heaven and against you. I am no longer worthy to be called your son.'

"But the father said to his servants, 'Quick! Bring the best robe and put it on him. Put a ring on his finger and sandals on his feet. Bring the fattened calf and kill it. Let's have a feast and celebrate. For this son of mine was dead and is alive again; he was lost and is found.' So they began to celebrate."

Every time I read this moving account of a father's love and yearning for his lost child, it brings me to tears because of the depth and width and length of the father's loving and tender forgiveness of his wayward child who has returned to his bosom. There was no scolding or "I told you so" from his father; no! He ran to his son, overjoyed to see his face once again! Do you get it? Father God is *not giving up on you!* He is searching for your return every day, always! If you turn to Him, He will run to you and take you up into His loving embrace. He will remove from you the filthy, ragged clothing of sin and give you a radiant white garment to wear and a ring that signifies you are once again under the protective covering of your Father's house. Hallelujah!

Once I laid this rebel's heart at the feet of my Father, Abba, He rescued and lifted me from the miry clay, setting my feet on solid ground. He took me from being battered by the world and thrown about by the waves of uncertainty, granting me stability, security, purpose, and peace beyond comprehension.

> I waited patiently and expectantly for the Lord;
>
> And He inclined to me and heard my cry.
>
> He brought me up out of a horrible pit [of tumult and of destruction], out of the miry clay,
>
> And He set my feet upon a rock, steadying my footsteps and establishing my path.

He put a new song in my mouth, a song of praise to our God;

Many will see and fear [with great reverence]

And will trust confidently in the Lord.

Blessed [fortunate, prosperous, and favored by God] is the man who makes the Lord his trust,

And does not regard the proud nor those who lapse into lies.

Many, O Lord my God, are the wonderful works which You have done,

And Your thoughts toward us;

There is none to compare with You.

If I would declare and speak of your wonders,

They would be too many to count.

Psalm 40:1–5

In time, God also restored to me the love and fellowship of my family members, bringing much-needed forgiveness and joy. Through the power of faithful prayers, God restored my older brother, who now has also turned from his prodigal lifestyle, returning to the arms of Jesus. Prayer also moved in the life of my youngest son, bringing him, his wife, and others in their family to the saving knowledge of the gospel of Jesus, also restoring and solidifying their marriage.

During the first few years of my renewed walk with the Lord, He granted me the immense privilege of adopting my amazing and beautiful daughter, Mary. She has blessed me with a wonderful grandson and granddaughter. I also was so blessed to serve as a foster parent to abused children for nearly four years. That is a whole other story in itself, but it doesn't stop here. God also led me to start a college career at the ripe age of forty-two. Being a single parent and relocating to Oklahoma midway through my pursuit delayed the completion of my degree, but I persisted. After ten years of study, with a major in sociology and a minor in psychology, I graduated from Oklahoma State University at the age of fifty-two!

My studies also included certification in human services, fostering a career as a social worker. God led me into a ten-year career as a certified domestic violence response professional. For the first seven years, I practiced in Florida, but upon moving to Oklahoma, I had the amazing experience of working in that field for two different Indian tribes, the Osage Nation and the Pawnee Nation. My work for the Pawnee Nation was in assisting them in founding a program to relieve the horrific effects of domestic violence and sexual assault from their reservation and the surrounding areas. Before starting these services, there was no such program available in that county. The program was built into a highly effective response system that has been embraced by the local communities and law enforcement, thereby reducing suffering and the fracturing of families and damage to its children in Pawnee County, Oklahoma.

One of the most liberating aspects of working for Native American tribes is that they are their own sovereign nation, not constrained by the misuse of "separation of church and state." I was free and even encouraged to share my faith and testimony to those whom I served, even praying with whoever was open to such relief. If you have faced subduing your testimony for Jesus in the workplace because it was disallowed, you might imagine how wonderful it was to be able to freely offer the *real* solution to the suffering and even to those who cause the suffering. Including the *power* of God in your efforts to change and repair a broken life is the only *lasting* solution to a shattered life, family, and community!

My story goes on. God just keeps amazing me! After years of failed relationships and marriages, the Lord brought together my husband and me about ten years ago. He was recovering from the death of his wife and the mother of his two teenage daughters. We had previously known one another in our high school band

and became reacquainted about a year after his late wife's passing. My dear husband, Barry, is the most generous, patient and wonderful man I have ever known. We share our faith in God, love of animals and family (our blended family consists of seven children, fifteen grandchildren, and eight great-grandchildren and counting)! We share an abundance of laughter in our beautiful home on a wooded three-acre property. Everyone loves coming to our home, sharing our sitting garden, and enjoying the peace of God's blessing here on this beautiful land.

I don't know why it took so many years to finally settle into God's rest, but I finally have, and plan on staying right here, spending splendid times with Him for the remainder of my days. I will continue in the privilege of serving Him and His kingdom, bringing glory to His wonderful Name!

It is very important for me to note here that although everything in my life has drastically changed for the better since surrendering to God's will, it hasn't excluded me from trials and heartaches. In the world, in its fallen state, a follower of Christ is not exempt from the troubles of this world; however, the power and presence of Holy Spirit in the life of every believer lift us to a higher level of strength, hope, and encouragement of spirit not available to an unbeliever.

Listen to what Jesus said about the challenges you face:

> "I have told you these things, so that in Me you may have [perfect] peace. In the world you have tribulation and distress and suffering, but be courageous [be confident, be undaunted, be filled with joy]; I have overcome the world." [My conquest is accomplished, My victory abiding.]
>
> John 16:33

My prayer is that you, too, will find your rest in the arms of Father God, *YHWH*, and be used by Him to bring the gospel of Jesus (His good news) to everyone, every step along the way!

"*[May] the Lord bless you and keep you; [may] the Lord make his face shine on you and be gracious to you; [may] the Lord turn his face toward you and give you peace*" (Numbers 6:24–26, NIV; emphasis added).

Amen.

CHAPTER 14
Finding the Common Thread

In What Manner Was the Occult Spread Throughout the World?

"Witchcraft" is a broad term, and commonly refers to "the use of magic," while magic itself can be defined as "the *manipulation and coercion* of hidden powers to act on specific events… or individuals, manipulating hidden powers in order to benefit or heal people or to cause them harm."[16]

In the following pages, the matters of witchcraft, sorcery, and the worship of spirits, goddesses, and other deities as practiced throughout the world and down through history are briefly outlined.

Common themes are woven throughout each society and period throughout history!

Witchcraft in Europe and Western Asia

The early Celts lived in an enormous region, stretching from modern day Turkey through eastern and central Europe and westward and northward into much of Spain, Portugal, France, Belgium, Britain and Ireland. This wide spread made a difference in the religion of the Celts in various regions. The Celts worshiped a variety of deities, male and female. Some of

---

16. Jonathan Burnside, "Covert Power: Unmasking the world of witchcraft," *Cambridge Papers* 19, no. 4 (2010). https://www.cambridgepapers.org/covert-power-unmasking-the-world-of-witchcraft (emphasis added).

these deities were associated with cosmos (sun, moon, stars), some with the local manifestations of the natural world (hills, rivers, wells, lakes, trees and mountains), others with cultural aspects such as wisdom and skill, healing and protection, magic, poetry, fertility and abundance.

The descriptions of the religions in Gaul are few. Three chapters of Caesar, a few lines from Diodorus, Mela, Strabo, Pliny and Lucian, and a statement from the Greek Timagenes, are reproduced in Ammianus Marcellinus. The preserved statues and inscriptions are also helpful. Caesar's Commentarii de bello Gallico tells that the concepts of the Celts regarding the gods *were much the same as others*, meaning the Romans and Greeks. He tells that the most worshipped god was Mercury; however, the Gauls' god was not named Mercury, but corresponded with the attributes of the Roman god. They regarded Mercury as the inventor of arts, presiding over trade and commerce, and the means of communication between people. After him, the Gauls honored Apollo, Mars, Jupiter, and Minerva. Of these gods, they held almost the same beliefs as the Romans did: Apollo drives away diseases, Minerva promotes handicrafts, Jupiter rules the heavens, and Mars controls war. Unfortunately, Caesar does not record the native names of the gods. In another article, Caesar records that the Gauls believe they are sprung from Pluto, the god of the lower world. This teaching comes from the Druids.

We have here the grim Teutates, Esus with fearful sacrifice, and Taranis, whose altars were no less grisly than those of Scythian Diana. There are statues of Esus, but not much can be said about him. Teutates was probably a war god, defender of people. Taranis was the god corresponding with the Norse god Thor. Lucian mentions another god Ogmios, the god of letters and eloquence. Other names mentioned in writings and inscriptions are Bel/Belenus-god of the Druids, sun and health, and Belisama- goddess of art.

One notable feature of Celtic sculpture is the frequent conjunction of male deity and female consort, a protective god with a mother-goddess who ensures the fertility of the land. These goddesses and mother-goddesses are identified with fertility and with the seasonal cycle of nature, and *both drew much of their power from the old concept of a great goddess, mother of all the gods.* Welsh and Irish traditions preserve many variations on a basic triadic relationship of divine mother, father, and son. The goddess appears, for example, in Welsh as Modron (from Matrona, "Divine Mother") and Rhiannon ("Divine Queen") and in Irish as Boann and Macha. Her partner is represented by the Gaulish father-figure Sucellos, his Irish counterpart Dagda, and the Welsh Teyrnon ("Divine Lord"), and her son by the Welsh Mabon (from Maponos, "Divine Son") and Pryderi and the Irish Oenghus and Mac ind Óg, among others.

Druids were a type of priesthood in the Celtic religion. The name itself means "knowing the oak tree" and may derive from druidic ritual. Caesar tells that the druids avoided manual labor and paid no taxes. As already mentioned, human sacrifice was practiced, but was forbidden by Tiberius and Claudius.[17]

Witchcraft in Africa

African witchcraft is not easy to define when you consider there are more than 50 different nations currently making up the diverse population of the continent. Not to mention the thousands of years of history on top of that. Basically, [it's] not really one single topic.

Many traditional African belief systems included different types of witchcraft and shamanism, but the influx of Christian missionaries have wiped out countless indigenous religions. Admittedly, some traditional beliefs considered witches to be evil in the first place but the addition of Christianity has added more negative associations even where there were none originally.

---

17. About History, "The Ancient Religion of the Celts—Celtic Polytheism," last modified July 10, 2023, https://about-history.com/the-ancient-religion-of-the-celts (emphasis added).

People are still burned for practicing witchcraft in some countries, not because of official law but rather by cultural practice. Aside from these issues, there are two forms of [magical] practice that people associate with African witchcraft: Santeria and Vodou.

Santeria

Most people associate Santeria with the Caribbean, which is accurate but it does also have deep roots in Western Africa. It is a blending of the original Yoruba religion from Africa, with many aspects of Roman Catholicism. This combination of beliefs arose from the slave trade, where Africans were taken to the various Caribbean islands to work. They adapted many Catholic beliefs, particularly the host of saints and created a unique religion that is still practiced there today.

In Santeria, there is a great Creator Deity but it is the Orishas that are directly worshiped. The Orishas are comparable to the Catholic saints, and they often have similar traits and characteristics. For example, Elegba and St. Anthony are closely connected as patrons over roads, transportation and gateways.

Though the saints are similar, the practices are very different from Catholicism. Santeria rituals often involve animal sacrifice along with vibrant dancing and drums. Offerings of food and alcohol are commonly associated with most Orisha.

Vodou

Though many people call it Voodoo, the more accurate name is Vodun or Vodou. It's a religion similar to Santeria as a mixture of Christian and African beliefs but it has gotten a lot more negative exposure from TV and movies. Vodou came from African with slaves and is primarily practiced in Haiti as well as some African nations.

There is one unknowable Deity figure, Olorun and the lesser spirits who are worshiped and prayed to are called the Loa (or the Lwa). Again, they are similar to many saints but the connection is not as strong as in Santeria.

Rituals in Vodou involve dancing and drumming and there is also sometimes animal sacrifice. Symbols called veves, drawn in various powders are used to call the Loa to the ritual.

These are both examples of African witchcraft, though they do not resemble the Wiccan form of witchcraft very much.[18]

The belief in witchcraft is widespread however. Witch doctors, who are meant to fight evil witchcraft, will assert that politicians belong to their good clients. Kofi Akosah-Sarpong, the author of the blog www.africanexecutive.com, reports from Ghana, that a study showed that 41 out of 45 medical students believed in witches—and that illnesses can be caused by sorcery.

This belief has devastating consequences. Even in advanced countries like Ghana and Kenya, people are often accused of being witches, persecuted and murdered. Especially the elderly, women and children become victims. In northern Ghana, there are so-called "witches' villages," where women accused of being witches seek shelter (Palmer 2010). UNICEF study pointed out that even children suffer violence as supposed witches in Africa, and some are killed (Cimpric, 2010). Between 1991 and 2001, around 22,500 Africans are said to have been lynched on the grounds of purportedly practicing witchcraft.[19]

According to my friend in Nigeria, Kelvin Ivara, a graduate student and minister of the gospel in Cross River, even today in Africa, witchcraft and sorcery are an everyday part of life. The following is his firsthand account of exposure to occult activity where he lives:

---

18. Free Witchcraft Spells, "African Witchcraft," accessed September 6, 2020, https://www.free-witchcraft-spells.com/african-witchcraft.html.
19. Helmut Danner, "Invisible Reality," D+C, April 24, 2013, https://www.dandc.eu/en/article/voodoo-and-witchcraft-africans-and-westerners-experience-religion-and-spirituality.

As I was registering for admission into the University of Calabar, I noticed, just at the main gate of the university, a group of about thirteen young men between the ages of fifteen and twenty-five years of age. They were arranging matchsticks; then they would beckon the new students to come and play the matchstick box game. As the new students pass by, some are enticed to gamble. Very strange; some gamble their entire tuition fee. I remember a theater and art student crying because he used the whole of his school fees to play the matchstick box game. From my observations, these young men who do the matchbox game use magic to deceive and manipulate people. So they start by enticing you with their tricks, and once you fall for it, they manipulate the game to their favor. "My son, if sinners entice you, Do not consent" (Proverbs 1:10).

Also, at the small gate of the same institution (known as Goldie by Mount Zion), there is a market adjacent to it. I saw another set of people controlling snakes and doing all sorts of magic to lure those passing by into witchcraft.

Now, this is how some of them are initiated into witchcraft. Notice they can't initiate or possess you or manipulate you without a connection. To make a connection, they put up posters of themselves and advertise, "I will make you rich and give you a ring for any woman to follow you. I will make your body strong enough for a bullet not to penetrate. I can help you to do soul travel. I can help you invoke money. I can help you connect with God." All these and more are their deceptions.

While I was growing up in Nigeria, I observed how many (especially the females) were being delivered from water spirit. However, some entangle themselves back and get possessed again. This witchcraft is the *ogbanje* mermaid spirit, usually from the coastal areas. It is rare in the northern part of Nigeria. The practice of divination is a belief passed on from ancestors. Some places still hold onto this norm today. For example, in Okrika's local government areas, there were places where they worship the water spirit. In those days when a woman could not conceive, the priests would take her to the river at midnight and perform some rites like bathing her and enchanting some spirit upon her.

In 2013, there was this particular church in Calabar where I was invited to play the keyboard and minister. I noticed for years the membership and strength of the church were not as expected, so the pastor was worried. Other churches are blooming with members, but his is scanty; even if this Sunday service has thirty-five members, the next one may have seventeen, while in comparison to other churches, they have members to the tune of five thousand and more, and it keeps growing!

Now, one of his friends, a fellow pastor, suggested to him that there was an oil, which he would have to buy for 200,000 naira, that he could use to inflict and heal sickness and do other things. (Let's be careful what we do when we are desperate in life.) Now, you see, that's how they deceive even Christians into witchcraft.

Politicians are not left out of witchcraft in Africa. They join some occult groups for personal gain, to get contracts, for protection, and for other benefits. Unfortunately, they forget whatever the devil gives he takes even much more in repayment.

Magic in East Asia

Magic and mantic arts are endemic in Chinese life and prominent in the religions of China, both in popular religion and in Buddhism and Daoism. The same is true of Korea and Japan, where indigenous beliefs have been overlaid by the cultural influence of China. The magical practices of China found ready acceptance in Korea and Japan. Although many of the practices traveled on their own, religion—chiefly Buddhism, which had already absorbed elements of Chinese popular beliefs and of Daoism—was an important vehicle for the transfer of Chinese magic. The result was an amalgam of magical lore in East Asia, with Chinese knowledge often providing a frame to which specifically Korean or Japanese practices and permutations were affixed.

China

In general, one should distinguish between magic, which provides a means to accomplish specific ends (through spells, gestures, amulets, talismans, and the like), and various occult sciences (such as yarrow-stalk divination with the Book of Changes, astrology, hemerology, geomancy, and alchemy), even though this distinction was not strongly maintained in the traditional Chinese schema of magic and the occult. There was in fact a fluid boundary between magic (where there was no cause for rationalization) and occult sciences, which were elaborated in terms of a theory of symbolic correspondence based on the concepts of *yin-yang* dualism and of Five Actions (*wuxing:* water, fire, wood, metal, and earth). Not only was this theory the product of prior conceptions of the magical power of fire, water, and other primary forces in nature (e.g., wind), but even after its full elaboration the symbolic correspondences did not negate the validity of magical practices. Not infrequently, occult theory supplied a *modus operandi* for magic and religious worship. For example, an astrological instrument designed to calculate the position of the Big Dipper (Chinese archaeology has recently brought to light a second-century BCE specimen of the device) was used by the usurper Wang Mang to direct the power of the Dipper against his enemies in 23 CE. From the beginning, this astrological instrument served as one means for conjuring the god of the Dipper and polestar (talismanic replicas of the constellation cast in metal were also used). The same instrument was influential in Daoist star magic, and it was the model for an astrological *mandala* in the esoteric Buddhism of the Tang period (618–907 CE). Similarly, the hemerological symbols of the calendrical cycle were not simply neutral signs marking the passage of time; they constituted a succession of spirits whose magical powers could be summoned through spells and talismans.

The Warring States (403–221 BCE), Qin (221–206 BCE), and Han (206 BCE–220 CE) periods were the formative age for Chinese magic. Earlier, magic was employed in dealings with the spirits and was important in the royal ancestral religion of the Shang and early Zhou (c. sixteenth–eighth centuries BCE). But the proliferation of magical arts, and an increasing differentiation between magic as employed in archaic religion and magic for its own sake, began during the Warring States and continued to develop in Qin-Han times. The history of Chinese magic in later centuries followed from the developments of this period. It was during the same period that the theory of symbolic correspondence was formulated, and developments in occult sciences paralleled significantly those in magic.

Before the Warring States the principal practitioners of magic were the *wu*, a class of female (and in lesser numbers, male) shamans who mediated between the human and spirit worlds. Their methods included trances in which spirits might descend into their bodies or in which the shaman might journey into the spirit world, invocations and maledictions, and the utilization of magical materials to either attract or repel the spirits. Their functions overlapped those of incantators (*chu*) and other ritual officiants; however, the latter did not engage in ecstatic trances. The Warring States and Qin-Han periods witnessed the decline in prestige of these shamans, who came to be increasingly associated with witchcraft; the rise of occult specialists (*fangshi*, literally "masters of recipes"), whose skills extended to magical operations; and the formation of a Daoist clergy, who adapted magic to fill the needs of the newly emergent religion (organized Daoist religious communities made their first appearance in the second century CE). The general populace also practiced forms of superstitious magic in the course of daily life.

Historical records of Han rulers who favored shamans and masters of recipes provide an important source of information about ancient Chinese magic. Liu Che (posthumously titled Wu Di; r. 140–87 BCE), for example, established cults for shamans and made his court a gathering place for masters of recipes who claimed to possess magical powers and the secrets of immortality. One master of recipes, Li Shaoweng, was a psychopomp who gained Liu Che's favor by conjuring the ghost of the ruler's recently deceased concubine; he was executed after he was exposed for fabricating portents. Near the end of Liu Che's reign the court was paralyzed by an outbreak of a type of shamanic witchcraft known as *gu*. The word *gu* referred to a demonic affliction that attacked its victim as the result of witchcraft. According to some accounts, *gu* was a poison produced by sealing certain creatures in a vessel until only one remained, which became the *gu*. The tradition that the *gu* is a magical potion cultivated by women and passed down through generations is still alive today. Those who ingested the *gu* were believed to die and become the demon-slaves of the *gu* and its keeper.

The Daoist sects that arose in the second century CE inveighed against those who placed their faith in shamans, worshiped demons, and believed the occultists' shams. These practices were an offense to the true deities of the Dao. Daoist liturgy incorporated many elements of popular worship, however, and the clergy engaged in many of the magical practices that they condemned in others. But in the continual process of syncretization that occurred over the centuries as Daoism interacted with popular religion and with Buddhism, the standard of orthodoxy fluctuated.

The Buddhist attitude toward magic was similar. Illicit magical practices fell under the category of the "arts of Mara" (*moshu*), Mara being the tempter and chief of malevolent demons. *Moshu* parallels other Chinese terms such as "shamanic arts" (*wushu*) and "way of the left" in referring to the forms of magic prohibited by the orthodox church (and the government). However, as early as the fifth century CE there was a tradition of Buddhist spell-casting in China rivaling the Daoist practices. Buddhist magic was most prominent in the esoteric practices of Tantrism. The Tantric literature contained magical formulas to be used to gain prosperity or harm adversaries; Tantric *mantras*, *mudrās*, and *mandalas* were utilized as instruments for working magic.

Tantric magic incorporated elements of native Chinese magic and occultism, while at the same time enriching Daoist and popular practices.

Many of the common forms of magic described in premodern sources are still practiced. There are spells to summon deities and to drive off demons (versions of popular, Daoist, and Buddhist spells are preserved). Spitting and spouting water over which a spell has first been uttered is another common device (sometimes Daoist or Buddhist priests will spout ignited alcohol). Substances believed to have magical properties are often identified in traditional materia medica.

Korea and Japan

In Korea, cults formed around female shamans were a source of native Korean magic. This popular religion is known as Mu-sok ("shamanic customs"). Contacts between Korea and China began well before the Tang, but increased markedly during that period. Knowledge of Chinese magic and occultism was part of the general flow of Chinese culture into Korea.

In the native religion of Japan, which came to be known as Shintō ("way of the spirits") after Buddhism took hold, there were two categories of religious personnel. The *miko* (female shaman) was a medium into whose body a spirit might descend, sharing essential characteristics with shamans throughout East Asia. The *kannushi* (spirit controller) was more in the nature of a priest who oversaw the worship of the spirits. As with the shamans in China, the *miko* were increasingly associated with witchcraft, whereas the *kannushi* came to function as officiants in the state cult. Esoteric tantric Buddhism had a strong influence in Japan, leading to a syncretism of Shintō and Chinese-Buddhist magic. Buddhist ascetics called *hijiri* (sage) and *yamabushi* (mountain recluse) traced their origins to the eighth century CE and were renowned for their magical powers. As in Korea, in Japan other forms of Chinese magic and occultism were absorbed into the culture.[20]

Kulam, the Philippines

Kulam is a form of sorcery that can be found in the Philippines, [centering] around islands like Siquijor and Talalora.

The witches that practice this magic are called mangkukulam, and they are often feared by people due to their reputation.

Kulam is heavily influenced by voodoo, which involves [utilizing] a doll to target their victims. The witches also have to obtain a personal belonging of their victim for their magic to work. Once a witch has obtained the required items, he or she will tie a string around the doll and recite an incantation. This awakens the spirits and allows the witch to have full control over the victim. Witches then have the power of hurting their victims through the doll. It is suspected that the only method of getting away from this voodoo curse is by either removing the string from around the doll or by killing the witch.[21]

Magic in Tibet

Bon, indigenous religion of Tibet that, when absorbed by the Buddhist traditions introduced from India in the 8th century, gave Tibetan Buddhism much of its distinctive character.

The original features of Bon seem to have been largely magic-related; they concerned the propitiation of demonic forces and included the practice of blood sacrifices. Later, there is evidence of a cult of divine kingship, the kings being regarded as manifestations of the sky divinity (reformulated in Buddhism as the reincarnation of lamas);

---

20. Encyclopedia.com, "Magic: Magic In East Asia," accessed September 10, 2020, https://www.encyclopedia.com/environment/encyclopedias-almanacs-transcripts-and-maps/magic-magic-east-asia.
21. Mariam Mohsen, "4 beliefs about witchcraft found in Asia," *Yahoo! Life*, September 12, 2016, https://sg.style.yahoo.com/4-interesting-witchcraft-rituals-in-asia-232102742.html.

an order of oracular priests (their counterpart, the Buddhist soothsayers); and a cult of the gods of the atmosphere, the earth, and subterranean regions (now lesser deities in the Buddhist pantheon).[22]

Slavic Witchcraft

Slavic folklore has plenty of similar stories about witches. According to the tradition, witches were able to heal people with herbs and magic, however, most of them were dangerous and malignant. Witches could be young women or old hags—like the phases of the moon, new moon, waning and waxing moon, and full moon; like the three archetypes of women: the young woman, the mature woman, and the crone.

Slavic witches, in general, had a bad reputation. They were haunting the wilderness at night, and lost travelers could see them dancing in the air in hailstorms. Witches were wandering in marshlands and moors, and they had some distinctive, strange, shimmering glow around them; these lights lured lost men—wood-cutters or hunters—right into the marsh, where, at last, the witch could drown them. The souls of these men have never found rest; they were lost forever. Witches could be seen near crossroads at midnight. They were able to bring down hailstorms in order to damage their enemies' property. They were associated with black cats and toads

Ghosts are an important part of Slavic tradition. There are plenty of Slavic superstitions dealing with ghosts. When someone could see a spot of steam on a glassy surface at night, it meant that there was an unseen—dead—person in the room, and the steam was left by its breathing. When the air cools in a room suddenly, or people can hear footsteps and noises that they cannot explain, then they knew their place was haunted. Haunting occurred in places where someone had died violently. Meeting a dead person usually meant

---

22. *Encyclopedia Britannica*, "Bon," last modified April 25, 2017, https://www.britannica.com/topic/Bon-Tibetan-religion.

nearing misery, supposedly the one who has seen the ghost would die in a short while.

Slavic—Russian, Ukrainian, Romanian—tradition also deals with werewolves and vampires. Werewolves were people who could turn into wolves and attack people. Vampires had glowing red eyes, one could not see their reflection in a mirror, they cast no shadows.[23]

Nordic Witchcraft

A Völva or as it is pronounced in old Norse a Vǫlva (in Danish a "Vølve"), is what we in English would call a Seeress. You could compare it to someone who practiced shamanism or witchcraft. So a Völva is a Nordic version of a shaman or witch, that practiced magic. The Völva in the Viking age were the predecessors of the medieval witches, so you could say, they were witches before it became cool. A Völva is not something that just dates back to the Viking age, a Völva is, in fact, very ancient, and their roots go back more than 2.000–3.000 years.

What Is a Völva

A Völva was a woman in the Viking age who practiced magic, known as Seidr (in old Norse seiðr), the word Seidr literally means "to bind." A Völva often had a very special role within the society and would often have close ties with the leaders of her clan. You could call a Völva/Vǫlva a spiritual leader or healer in the Nordic society. A man could also practice Seidr, and he would be known as a Seer, but that was very rare.

A Völva wore colorful dresses, which as I said before would probably have been the same for both male and females. She would also wear gloves and a hat made from cat fur, and have a beautiful decorated staff or wand. The staff or wand was an important accessory in the carrying out Seidr.

---

23. Meet the Slavs, "Slavic Folklore—Vila's, Witchcraft and Mythical Creatures," accessed September 8, 2020, https://meettheslavs.com/slavic-folklore.

The staff was very important to the Völva, her staff was actually so important to her that the word Völva probably means staff or wand carrier.

The people were afraid of a Völva because she possessed a lot of power and the knowledge of magic. A Völva would not always live a long life, the practice of magic was dangerous and moving back and forth between dimensions/realms, had many unforeseen consequences. But her death could also be caused by her own clan if they did not like her prophesies.

A Völva was also able to leave her own body and enter into an animal, it is uncertain how or why she would do that, but it might have been to travel great distances, for instance to another town or place to observe and gather knowledge. The practice of Seidr was mostly used to do good and help the people, and Seidr was not just used in rituals to contact the spirits, it was also used on daily basis, it could be used to heal wounds, create happiness or to control the weather.

But the practice of Seidr could also be used in a more sinister way, what we today would call black magic. Seidr could be used to put a curse on a person or make someone deadly ill. Seidr could also be used to bind the will of the warriors in a battle, make them slow, disoriented, and in that way indirectly be guilty of their death.[24]

Witchcraft in Germany

On April 30th for Walpurgisnacht, witches, warlocks, and wizards gather for the Great Sabbath of the year. Some fly to the meeting places on their brooms or forks, others turn themselves into cats, goats, horses, and toads for the journey, some leave their bodies and attend the meeting in spirit, while others cover their bodies with a secret ointment to grow bat wings so they can fly to the gathering. In their place, they leave a *vicarium daemonem*, their demonic double. It doesn't matter which method is used for traveling, as long as the meeting is honored by everyone's presence.

---

24. Nordic Culture, "Völva the Viking Witch or Seeress," last modified March 11, 2018, https://skjalden.com/volva-the-viking-witch-or-seeress.

They gather just before midnight at crossroads, mountain tops, and in forests, they light a roaring bonfire which they jump through and dance around, until their Horned God arrives in their middle and the true Night of the Witches begins. They commune with their god and make love to him, they release their magic *to defend it against the rising cross which with its shadow darkened the light of ancient magic.* The Witches' Sabbath is the conversion of ancient Dionysiac mysteries to a Christian context. The ancient fertility rites which were Dionysiac in nature were performed in the cover of the night, when the fire was brighter and when the aphrodisiacs were stronger.

The priestess performing these rites were accompanied by men disguised as mythical figures with horns and hooves, such as Faunus or Pan, and they partied for their gods, such as the drunk god, Silenus, and the horseman god, Sabazios. The priests and priestesses attending the Dionysiac celebrations covered their bodies with magical ointments which gave them vivid dreams, hallucinations, or a profound sleep. The secret recipes of these ointments survived through the Dark Ages, guarded by the witches who participated in the Great Sabbath.

Before they went to sleep on the Night of the Witches, they covered their body with these secret ointments, which gave them visions of fire, flying witches, and horned gods. In the Middle Ages, many witches testified to the sensation of flight given by some of these ointments that contained narcotics and poisonous herbs. The Inquisition tried to find out the recipes for these secret ointments, and the witches who confessed did so using code names for the ingredients they used. Ingredients like baby fat, bat blood, opium, and mandrake fed the imagination of the public that witches were evil creatures that kidnapped children to use them for their [sabbats].

Walpurgisnacht is the greatest of all [sabbats] throughout the year, it is a night of "bewitched bodies" that "glow with flames through and through," of "werewolves and dragon women passing by in flight" (Die erste Walpurgisnacht), when witches fly on their brooms to mountain tops where they conjure the ancient magic of the old gods. Although the Christian Church has tried to overturn the old celebration by trying to establish a Christian patron that protects against witches on the very night of the witches, the essence of this celebration is still there and perhaps nowadays it's embraced for what it is more than in the previous centuries.[25]

Psychic and Mystical Experiences of the Aborigines [in Australia]

Only since the 1950s have anthropologists understood that religion and the Dreamtime myths are at the core of Aboriginal society…Only recently have Aborigines written or recommended books that accurately portray their own culture…Many Aboriginals now prefer the traditional name Koori, as used in central New South Wales.

Interaction for trade and ceremony has produced a common set of basic religious beliefs about the Dreamtime. Their basis is an essential unity and harmony between humans, the land and the Dreamtime. The arid climate made a close bond with the land essential. One's birth place is seen as the essential link with the inner self (the spirit world). Aborigines are thus very attached to their sacred sites, and they feel alienated when displaced from their homeland into cities.

The Dreamtime

The term Dreamtime was first used in 1896 by Spencer and Gillen as a rough translation of the Aranda term "alcheringa." Aborigines later adopted "Dreamtime" as their own word. Other tribes use words such as bugari, djugurba, tjukurpa, wongar and ungud. The Dreamtime is at least three things in one:

A sacred heroic time long ago when spirit beings set the <u>sun, moon and stars</u> in their courses, and created the earth, material

---

25. The Old Craft, "Walpurgisnacht—Or: Walpurgis' Night—The Witch's Flight to the Great Sabbath," last modified April 29, 2018, https://www.theoldcraft.com/2018/04/29/walpurgisnacht-or-walpurgisnight-the-witchs-flight-to-the-great-sabbath (emphasis added).

life and spiritual life. The spirits also created laws (rituals) to provide meaning and to perpetuate this way of life.

The storage of spirit power into plants, animals and sacred sites, for example, a rocky outcrop or waterhole. It provides a meaning for, and a way of life both to individuals and society.

The term "The Dreaming" refers to an Aboriginal's awareness and knowledge of the Dreamtime. The term "dream" is a metaphor suggesting that awareness is enhanced by dreamy, quiet, vague, visionary, fantasy or trance states. The land and ritual serve as reminders; monuments and churches are not needed.

Mystical Experience

Stanner states that Aboriginal beliefs were mystical. In 1977 Elkin [recognized] that the Dreaming would today in part, be called a mystical or spiritual experience. The Dreamtime myths also contain fragmented memories of early Aboriginal history. In an Arnhem Land myth, the creator spirit came from "over the sea," consistent with archaeological evidence for their arrival from SE Asia 40,000 years ago.

Tribes can be distinguished by their Dreamings. Aboriginals believe there is a "oneness of person, body, spirit, ghost, shadow, name, spirit site and totem." The Dreamtime is not an historic event. It corresponds to the whole of reality. It has a beginning, but is eternal the Aborigines have no word for abstract "time." The Dreaming is a "vertical line in which the past underlies and is within the present." The power of the Dreaming is still available, as shown by Christian religious conversion of the Wonajagu people in 1963. Knowledge of sacred sites is secret and imparted to few. The Dreamtime is a "unity of waking-life and dream-life." For example, to conceive, a man first finds a child in his "dreams," and directs it to his wife. An artist produces a new song by dream contact with a spirit.

Spirit Beings and Totems

There are two categories of spirit beings.

A few all-powerful transcendental beings who created the earth. Often called All-Father. An example; the Sky Beings, called Baiame in New South Wales and Bunjil in Victoria. The Wondjina, primal beings of the Kimberley District, are depicted with halos in huge paintings.

Numerous lesser spirits belonging to single tribes. [Symbolized] in the material world as animal or plant totems. Examples; The Lightning Brothers, and the Red Kangaroo Man. Most spirits are good but some are bad, such as the Bunyip who lives in swamps and billabongs (cut-off stream branches). Two types of tribal spirits exist: eternal (from the Dreamtime); and human (spirits of the dead). The latter leave the body and return to their "home" (the sky, an island, or cave); they may return to haunt people. The Rainbow Serpent the rainbow personified—is a myth bridging both categories. He arrived soon after All-Father, and carved the valleys and hills with his writhing body.

Myth and Ritual

The link to the Dreaming is reinforced by rituals and ceremonies (corroborees)—stories, dancing and singing during which an Aboriginal acts as, and becomes, a spiritual being or totem. Myth and the rituals of art, song and dance reinforce each other. The main myths, guiding all aspects of life, concern life, death, rebirth and fertility. The myths involve the actions of spirits, and their travel between sacred sites.

Medicine Men

All Aboriginals can outline these myths but only a few men—or rarely, women—are told the meaning of the most sacred myths. This is the medicine man, man of high degree, clever man or shaman.

A medicine man is selected because of a history of trances and visions. Medicine men initiate new recruits with magic rituals involving spirit beings. Rituals involve fear, isolation and suggestion. He may prepare for initiation by a two-month fast. He may be given "new insides," and quartz crystals may enter his body to provide power. He is given magic (astral) rope enabling him to fly through the air (have an out-of-body experience or OBE). He acquires X-ray vision from maban stones.

Healing and Divining

There are two types of medicine man; diviner-doctor (who heals) and sorcerer (who creates illness). The same man may play both roles. Power is drawn from faith, ritual and special knowledge of the Dreaming. The exact techniques do not matter. The main point is that it is believed.

Healing involves songs or spells, in the presence of quartz crystals, tektites, shells or special stones. Techniques include sleight of hand, ventriloquism, massaging and sucking, and acute perception and hearing. Divining involves consulting the spirits of the recent dead to find if sorcery or murder was involved. The diviner can then cast counter-spells.

Sorcery and Voodoo Death

The sorcerer casts spells onto victims or their goods ("singing," at times to death). He can inflict bad luck or injury by look alone ("evil eye"). Kadaicha men lead avenging expeditions involving pointing the bone. The victim is stunned or speared and magical operations are performed on him. The bone is magically projected into the victim's body. Blood or the soul is withdrawn from the body along a magic cord (as in "psychic surgery.")

From 1969 to 1980, a psychiatrist studied Aboriginal men in Arnhem Land. Sorcery syndrome (gross fear of death) was common. Symptoms were agitation, sleeplessness, visions and protruding eyeballs. Fear was precipitated by trauma, for example, death or serious illness of a close relative, or a dispute over wives. A few victims died. The victim was outcast and deprived of water; thus dehydration rather than fright may have caused death.

Psychic Experiences

Starting in the Kimberleys in the 1930s, Elkin collected many reports of psychic phenomena, later published as a book in 1944. Medicine men supposedly had such powers at will; they were excellent magicians. Ordinary Aboriginals had them only at times, such as on the death of a relative. Psychic abilities resulted from openness to experience, lack of attention to time, and the quiet and solitude of the bush. Anecdotes included seeing spirits, healing (in part, psychic surgery), sorcery, telepathy over huge distances, X-ray vision, sending the "dream familiar" out of the body (OBE), hypnotism, and fire-walking. Prophecy is rare.

Until Europeans arrived, the Aborigines used few drugs. The main one was pituri from the shrub Duboisia hopwoodii. The active ingredient is nicotine, the same alkaloid as in tobacco. "Pituri" is also used more broadly to include wild tobacco weed. The chemistry of pituri differ widely. In the Northern Territory, the drug is actually non-nicotine, four times more toxic than nicotine. Aborigines there prefer tobacco weed.

Aborigines used pituri to inspire mirth, to increase stamina and courage before warfare or firewalks. Pituri can induce trances, thus accessing the Dreamtime, that is psychic and mystical experiences. Nicotine is also commonly used in American shamanism.

Pituri also refers to the dried leaves and stems of the shrub. Aborigines smoke "quid," a mixture of leaves with ash from the acacia bush, thus increasing drug potency. Leaves are placed behind the ear, or on other body parts. Nicotine is absorbed through the skin. Nicotine in quid -three times more concentrated than in cigarettes—produces stupor and catalepsy, a trancelike pain-free state.

Pituri is hoarded and the shrub localities kept secret. It grows over much of Western Queensland, Eastern Northern Territory and Northwestern NSW, where it was widely traded.

Pituri can induce trances, thus accessing the Dreamtime, that is, psychic and mystical experiences.[26]

Modern Witchcraft

Stregheria is a branch of modern paganism that celebrates early Italian witchcraft. Its adherents say that their tradition has pre-Christian roots, and refer to it as *La Vecchia Religione*, the Old Religion. There are a number of different traditions of Stregheria, each with its own history and set of guidelines.

Today, there are many pagans of Italian descent who follow Stregheria. The website Stregheria.com, which bills itself as "the home of Stregheria on the web," says,

"Catholicism served as a veneer that was fitted over the Old Religion in order to survive during the period of violent persecution at the hands of the Inquisition and secular authorities. To many modern Italian Witches, most Catholic saints are simply ancient pagan gods dressed in Christian garb."

Charles Leland and Aradia

Stregheria appears to be based primarily upon the writings of Charles Leland, who published "Aradia: Gospel of the Witches" in the late 1800s. Although there's some question about the validity of Leland's scholarship, "Aradia" continues to be the basis of most Stregheria traditions. The work purports to be a scripture of an ancient pre-Christian witch cult, passed along to Leland by a woman named Maddalena.

According to Maddalena, by way of Leland, this tradition honors Diana, the moon goddess, and her consort, Lucifer… Together, they had a daughter, Aradia, and she comes to earth to teach people the ways of magic.

---

26. The Australian Institute of Parapsychological Research, "Psychic and Mystical Experiences of the Aborigines," accessed April 13, 2024, https://www.aiprinc.org/aboriginal.

To some degree, this *teaching is focused on enlightening peasants as to how to overthrow their tyrannical masters and find freedom in escaping from societal and economic constraints.*

[*By the way, does this teaching remind you of what was happening in the USA, in places like Portland, Oregon, during the George Floyd protests?*]

Leland's material gained in popularity among Italian Americans during the 1960s, but his work was not the only influence on what is today practiced as Stregheria. During the 1970s, author Leo Louis Martello, who was open about his practice of Italian witchcraft, wrote numerous titles detailing his family's practice of magic originating in Sicily. According to Sabina Magliocco, in her essay "Italian American Stregheria and Wicca: Ethnic Ambivalence in American Neopaganism,"

"While the secret nature of his family magical practice made it impossible for him to reveal all its characteristics, he described it as a remnant of Sicily's cult of Demeter and Persephone, preserved under the guise of Marian worship in the Catholic Church. In fact, he claimed *that Sicilian families concealed their pagan religion under the guise of devotion to the Virgin Mary, whom they interpreted as simply another version of the goddess Demeter.*"[27]

Magic and Sorcery in Ancient Rome and Greece

For the Greeks magic (*mageia* or *goeteia*) was a wide-ranging topic which involved spells and evil prayers (*epoidai*), curse tablets (*katadesmoi*), enhancing drugs and deadly poisons (*pharmaka*), amulets (*periapta*) and powerful love potions (*philtra*). The modern separation of magic, superstition, religion, science, and astrology was not so clear in the ancient world. This mysterious, all-encompassing art of magic was [practiced] by both male and female [specialized] magicians who people sought out to help them with their daily lives and to overcome what they saw as obstacles to their happiness.

---

27. Learn Religions, "What Is Stregheria?" last modified May 20, 2018, https://www.learnreligions.com/about-stregheria-traditions-2562552 (emphasis added).

Practitioners of *mageia*, the magicians, the first of whom, to the Greeks at least, were the Magi (*magoi*) priests of Persia, were seen not only as wise holders of secrets but also as masters of such diverse fields as mathematics and chemistry. Associated with death, divination, and evil-doing magicians were, no doubt, feared, and their life on the fringes of the community meant that practitioners were often impoverished and reliant on handouts to survive.

Magic in Greek Mythology

Magic appears in the mythology of ancient Greece and was associated with such figures as Hermes, Hecate (goddess of the moon and witchcraft), Orpheus, and Circe, the sorceress daughter of Helios who was expert in magical herbs and potions and who helped Odysseus summon the ghosts from Hades. Myths abound in tales of magic potions and curses. Just one example is Hercules, who died a horrible death after his wife Deianeira had taken the magic blood of the centaur Nessos and liberally spread it on the hero's cloak. On wearing it, Hercules was burned terribly and would later die of his wounds. Magic is also [practiced] by many literary characters, perhaps most famously by Medea in Euripides' tragedy play of the same name.

Who Believed in Magic?

Magic in the Greek world was not just prevalent in the realm of private individuals, neither was it reserved for the poor and illiterate. We know that official inscriptions were commissioned by city-states to protect their city from any possible disasters. There were also cases when, as at Teos in the 5th century BCE, the state delivered the death penalty to a man and his family found guilty of harmful magic (*pharmaka deleteria*). In another example, a 4th-century BCE woman by the name of Theoris received the death sentence for distributing bewitching drugs and incantations. Clearly, the authorities [recognized] magic as an activity capable of results and it was not simply the realm of weak-minded peasantry. Certainly, some intellectuals [realized] its potential for abuse, as in the case of Plato who wanted to punish those who sold spells and curse tablets.

It is interesting to note that while magicians in mythology are often female the records of curse tablets and spells typically indicate a male user. Curse tablets were mostly used as a means to settle disputes in one's [favor]. The first record of them dates to the 6th century BCE and they cover such topics as business deals, relationship problems, legal disputes, cases of revenge, and even athletic and drama competitions. There are instances in Greek literature where entire families and dynasties are cursed, perhaps the most famous being Oedipus and his descendants.

Magic Spells

The Egyptians had long used spells (really better described as a list of instructions to follow) and incantations written on papyri and the Greeks continued the tradition. Surviving Greek papyri concerning magic date to the 4th and 3rd century BCE. They cover such instructions as how to get over physical ailments, improve one's sex life, exorcism, eliminate vermin from the home, as parts of initiation ceremonies, or even how to make your own amulet. Recipes and poisons frequently appear too, which often used rare herbs and exotic ingredients such as spices and incense from distant Asia.[28]

Witchcraft in Ancient Italy and Greece

The Eleusinian Mysteries are a set of traditions that have been practiced for 2000 years. The popular pseudo-religion invited all, accepting slaves, women, and men, regardless of financial standing and background.

The origin of the group centers on a conflict between Greek gods...

---

28. World History Encyclopedia, "Magic in Ancient Greece," last modified July 26, 2016, https://www.worldhistory.org/article/926/magic-in-ancient-greece.

The Origins of the Eleusinian Mysteries

The longest lasting "mystery" religion of the Greco-Roman period spanned nearly 2000 years, extending out of Mycenean traditions (approx. 1500 BC) and the Greek Dark Ages. The Eleusinian Mysteries are named for their origin in the city of Eleusis, but the religion centers on the story of Demeter, the goddess of agriculture, and her daughter Persephone. One day, Persephone is captured by Hades. In order to coerce the other Greek gods to retrieve Persephone from the Underworld, Demeter causes a worldwide drought.

The drought deprives humans of food—but, more importantly, the Greek gods of sacrifices. Zeus orders Hades to return Persephone, but a dirty rule of the Underworld calls for anyone who consumes food within the Underworld to stay within its boundaries forever. Persephone ate several pomegranate seeds during her stay in Underworld, but a deal is struck that calls for her to return to Hades for four to six months out of the year, months when Demeter will be dissatisfied and once again prohibit the growth of plants. This story of Demeter and Persephone sets forth an understanding of the change in seasons against a backdrop of the Greek pantheon.

Initiation and Secret Knowledge

The cult of Demeter and Persephone allowed anyone in society to enter, as long as the individual spoke Greek and never committed murder. The individual's station in life did not matter — slaves, women, and the poor could enter into the group and access the fellowship and secret knowledge of the Eleusinian Mysteries. The Eleusinian Mysteries featured a series of celebrations consisting of Lesser Mysteries and Greater Mysteries, with the Greater celebrated every five years or so. Most details of the mysteries did not survive to today, as members who revealed the more elusive secrets often met their demise at the hands of other members. The secrets of the mysteries are thought to revolve around hidden physical objects — the contents of a giant chest and an enclosed basket are known by low level imitates, with an increasing number of secrets revealed to tenured members and priests.

The Greatest Mystery and a Psychedelic Twist

The most important ritual for those involved in the Eleusinian Mysteries involved a ten day journey to Eleusis and a fast broken by drinking kykeon. The administration of kykeon, a peasant drink consisting of barley and the common cooking herb pennyroyal, is a subject of controversy for modern historians, as the kykeon served near the end of the journey likely contained a psychoactive ingredient.

Ergot, a parasite that grows on barley, emits ergometrine and d-lysergic acid amide, a chemical precursor to LSD that exhibits similar psychedelic effects and a DEA schedule III drug in the United States. After ingesting the kykeon, the participant enters the final portion of the journey, wherein the most secret aspects of the mystery are revealed, with many experiencing visions pertaining to the possibility of eternal life. The influence of mind altering drugs is believed to bolster the individual's reaction to the final step and help the Eleusinian Mysteries survive for nearly two thousand years against a plethora of other mystery cults and the rise of Christianity in Rome.

Like many mystery cults of the time, the influx of Christianity and Christian emperors of Rome led to the downfall of the Eleusinian rituals.[29]

---

29. Keith Veronese, "The Psychedelic Cult That Thrived For Nearly 2000 Years," *Gizmodo*, February 10, 2012, https://gizmodo.com/the-psychedelic-cult-that-thrived-for-nearly-2000-years-5883394.

Milton Keynes UK
Ingram Content Group UK Ltd.
UKHW022251051124
450708UK00014B/1067